MIRAGE

How Social Media Impacts The Way We Think, Feel, And Behave

TYLER HENDON

CONTENTS

Dedicated to my sister, Ewanda.

For believing in me before I believed in myself.

1

SHOW AND TELL

I WAS BORN in the early '90s on a warm summer day in Detroit, Michigan. My mother and grandmother raised me on the west side of the city. They both taught me invaluable life lessons. My grandmother was a nurturer, and my mother was the provider and leader for the family. They poured into me daily, loved me dearly, and did their best to steer me in the right direction.

Our home was in the center between two drastically different houses. To our left, an abandoned home. When the owner of that house passed away, the property was left to rot. I remember the grass at that house growing so tall that my mother sometimes paid to have it mowed. I watched that home decay as I grew into my teenage years.

To our right, a home that belonged to a man we'll call Steve. Steve was a car aficionado. Steve and his friends were known around the neighborhood for having a ton of cars. What they did to buy those cars is a story for another day, but the truth remains, they had *a lot* of cars. Benz', Lexus', Cadillacs, Hummers—you name it, they bought it.

My favorite was Steve's 2002 Lexus SC 430. It was cherry red with a convertible top, spinning rims, and beige leather seats. It was an amazing car, and he took great care of it. I tried my best to stay away from Steve, but I can guarantee you I got a bit closer whenever he started to wash that beautiful car!

Steve and his friends bought designer clothes and shiny jewelry. Some of them wore pristine, expensive Cartier glasses and virtually all of them wore the latest Air Jordan sneakers.

In those days, if you wanted to see luxury, you had to see it in person or on TV. The internet wasn't a "thing" quite yet. At that time, we couldn't hop on Instagram and enter the world of the rich (or seemingly rich) through photos and videos of their homes, cars and jewelry. These days, luxury is in your face at all times.

Twenty-four hours, seven days a week, we're exposed to it. It's easily accessible on your phone, TV, computer, and tablet. This increased exposure has had an impact on our culture—which leads us into the main point of this chapter.

PEOPLE FEEL MORE PRESSURE THAN EVER TO KEEP UP WITH OTHER PEOPLE. WE CAN COMPARE EVERY PART OF OUR LIVES TO OTHER PEOPLE'S SOCIAL MEDIA HIGHLIGHTS. In addition, materialism is at an all-time high. The emergence of the internet and social media have played a huge role in intensifying people's desire to *look* like they are well off. We want to be perceived as happy, healthy, and successful, even if none of them are true.

Since the beginning of time, men have competed for the spot of top dog. "Keeping up with the Joneses" is an old phrase representing people's desire to accumulate material possessions to show they are just as good, if not better, than their neighbors. This is nothing new! Many of us try our hardest to keep up with our friends, family, and peers. The key difference now is—today, our neighborhood is global.

We can compare our Real Lives with the online lives of others. We can compare our one-bedroom apartments to the $60-million Kardashian mansions in California. We can compare our hourly jobs to the lavish careers of rockstars. We can compare our quiet, Netflix-filled weekends to the fun, exciting and Instagram worthy weekends of our peers.

These comparisons come with consequences. One consequence we face is an increased desire to *show* what we have and feeling like we're *less* when we don't have the things we think we should. These comparisons create more room for us to feel insecure, jealous and unfulfilled, amongst other emotions.

Like many people, the "Steves" of 2021 are much louder than they were in 2002. They have more ways to share their excess. The rise of social media has given them, and every one of us, more platforms on which to share the things we accumulate. Many people's desire to shine has skyrocketed. That "shine" can be anything from our new home, our beautiful family, our great job or our luxurious travel. In fact, some people want to shine so badly that they are willing to risk anything or do anything to receive those "likes" and validation.

I don't blame them for being a bit misguided. In many ways, we connect most with the things we think we need to feel whole. Even if they don't realize it, many are enamored with this idea that they need material possessions to be validated. For some that means riches.

In my culture, which blends with hip-hop culture, we glorify wealth—everything from Patek Philippe Watches, Hermes Birkin bags, and Lamborghini trucks. Instagram "Car Reveals" as I like to call them, can quickly make you feel like you need more and create confusion around everyday people's access to wealth.

Seeing these images over and over creates a *Mirage* that can lead one to believe luxury is readily available. This is the opposite of the truth: luxury is rare and unattainable for the great majority of people throughout the world and the US is no exception. In fact, the majority of the world's wealth is owned by a small amount of people. This is common knowledge, but depending on the content on our timeline, we may not see this reality when we visit social media.

Some of us have what I like to call, "financial-esteem." Financial-esteem can be defined as confidence and self-worth that is closely tied to one's financial status. In this instance, we directly tie money to our *value*.

A person with a high financial-esteem feels great as long as the cash is flowing. When the money goes, their confidence and self-worth take a hit. The reason being that their *confidence* is connected to their financial status in an unhealthy way. There are often other factors that affect their confidence (culture, ethnicity, background, education, faith), but a significant piece of their confidence is tied to their finances.

Today, our values are too closely tied to our money and the endless list of things we can spend money on. We can spend money on everything from a new body to a dream vacation. If our values are too closely tied to our finances, we risk feeling unhappy and deprived if and when we go through financial hardship. In a way, this is the nature of the world we live in. Any one of us can fall into this space.

It is much easier to feel confident and worthy when you have money in your pocket, as opposed to when you don't. It's easier to be happy and comfortable when you aren't struggling to pay your bills or worried about your next meal.

The difference is that today, if we're down on our luck, we can be constantly reminded that we're *down*. If we just lost our job, we can login to LinkedIn and see a friend post about their new dream job at Google. If we just left our relationship, we can login to Instagram and see people getting married, buying homes together, starting seemingly perfect families, and taking "baecations."

Social media creates another lane for us to feel and know that our life isn't perfect.

For many reasons, we smile a bit bigger when our lives are comfortable. When our relationships are going well, we feel more peace. These are natural, healthy occurrences but social media makes it harder to be on the opposite end of those situations.

When we log on, we're able to see infinite images of wealth that very few of us will ever obtain. We see positions, opportunities, and places that many of us won't experience. The images are *free* to view but come at a cost: we begin to compare our lives to what we see online.

I often worry about people who don't truly know the difference between what they see online and what is Real Life. Some of these people are young; some are full-grown adults. I wonder how many of us know that we are looking into a *Mirage*, an illusion that appears real but may not be. In my teens, I wasn't constantly bombarded online with lavish lifestyles and the idea that there are a ton of people with picture-perfect lives.

The pressure to have "things" can be dangerous and is at an all-time high.

I distinctly remember buying my first car. It was the summer of 2010. I was 19 years old. That summer, I lived in Chicago and worked full-time for ComEd, an electric services company. My father allowed me to stay with him rent-free. He cooked, bought groceries, and encouraged me to save money. I think he wanted to make sure I was set for my sophomore year of college. I was, and still am, very fortunate to have him as a dad.

My only issue with my father is that he didn't allow me to buy a Chrysler 300 with black tinted windows and 22-inch rims. I would've felt very cool riding in that car at 19 years old. One day I'll let it go, but it won't be today!

My first car was a 2001 Buick Regal. It had silver paint, new headlights, and a cloth interior. I paid the owner a flat three grand, all cash. I was satisfied but not truly happy. I wanted more.

A piece of me felt like I *needed* to shine a bit brighter. I wanted a car that could rival one of Steve's cars. At the time, I wanted big rims, a sound system and any other additions that were supposed to make me feel successful.

Soon after I bought the car, I washed, waxed, and cleaned it from bumper to bumper. I vacuumed the inside, scrubbed the seats and hung air freshener to give it that "new car smell." The car didn't look half bad. A few days later, I went to visit my best friend, Jalon. Jalon, who spent five years in the US Army, was very happy for me. He told me everything that he loved about the car.

He picked out small things to *show* me how happy he was for me. Jalon's older brother James did the same. James complimented the car and told me that I did a good job.

I wasn't too high on myself or the car, so I responded quietly, "Yeah, it's cool." At that moment, James saw that I wasn't very happy with my purchase. James looked at me then looked back at the car. He then looked me in my eye and said, "That's exactly where you're supposed to be. Don't let anyone tell you different." At the time, this seemed like a nice thing to say. It made me feel a bit more comfortable with my car—having someone I admired reaffirm my decision was a great feeling.

As I reflect on it now, I can see James knew something as a young man that many of us tend to forget.

Sometimes we're exactly where we need to be, even if we feel that we should have more.

Remember, there will always be more. There will always be a situation that looks better than yours. There will always be a nicer "thing" to obtain. Social media shows us nicer things constantly. Let's say you want a new TV. Through a social media algorithm or an iPhone agreement you probably didn't read, you'll stumble across one on your timeline. Soon enough, your timeline will throw TVs at you. You will see ads for TVs of every brand, size, and screen resolution.

It can be difficult at times, but it's our job to discern between what we actually need and what we can go without. There will always be *more*, but the *more* isn't going anywhere. Trust me.

Please remember that you don't need the next best thing to feel whole. It took me a while to learn this lesson, about 26 years if I'm being honest, but it's 100 percent true. The people that truly love you will love you whether your clothes are from Walmart or from Gucci. When you look online, you'll see people dressed from head to toe in fancy clothes, sitting in powerful positions, driving luxurious cars and taking extravagant trips. These images are rampant online and prevalent in pop culture.

Remember, very few people on earth live a life of luxury; in fact, millions of people around the world struggle to make ends meet— and those numbers only rose once COVID-19 emerged. Many people on this planet live their life in a constant state of survival, fighting for their next meal and a roof over their head.

Do your best to be thankful for what you have, even if you believe it isn't much. At times, log off, pursue your passions, and ensure your head and heart aren't being steered toward believing you must have more stuff or be in a different situation to be happy.

All of this is to say, I'm guilty of falling into the trap of believing that I always needed *more*. I've blown money trying to keep up with other people—some I barely knew! After finishing college, I lived in a few different places throughout the country, but I always found time to visit my family and friends in Detroit. After I started to make decent money, I rented a nice car every single time I visited the city. I rented BMW's, Benz's and plenty of muscle cars.

Even if the trip was for two days, I rented a car. I rented cars that I didn't even know how to start. I blew so much money that my uncle told me to slow down!

At that time, I spent much more than I should have on designer clothes and material things.

Like many, there were times when I bought new things because I liked them and wanted to update my wardrobe. At other times, these purchases acted as a cape to cover my own insecurities and self-doubt. I sometimes felt incomplete, but as long as I looked the part, no one would know, right? In hindsight, those decisions helped me grow and were *truly* a phase.

At the time, those decisions didn't make me happier with who I was, but they did help me learn this:

Humans need balance.

There's nothing wrong with having nice things, but there needs to be a certain understanding of the value those things hold in our life. Social media culture can make it hard for us to find that understanding.

Whether we want to have a new set of porcelain-white teeth, a picture-perfect body, or a Dior outfit, we must realize that we don't really *need* these things, but it is okay to want them and to obtain them.

Wanting more out of life is normal and healthy! You *should* want to be successful and enjoy your success. You *should* want financial security, a healthy family, and a happy home. It is OK if you want that new Prada purse (or man bag if you're into that). It is very normal to want nice things, and it is normal to enjoy having nice things.

Just remember, regardless of what you may see on the internet, your worth as a human being is not tied to the things you accumulate. It is not tied to how much money you have, how many people like your posts, the trips you take, or what other people say about you—period. Many of us, including myself, are guilty of attaching who we are to what we have. Be very careful about connecting your humanity to vanity.

2

PEOPLE WILL NOT FORGIVE YOU

IN UNDERGRAD, I developed relationships with some amazing people. One of them, who we'll call Floyd, became one of my close friends. Around that time, it was clear to me that Floyd would become successful. Floyd graduated with a bachelor's degree in Supply Chain Management from Michigan State, which has one of the best Supply Chain Management programs in the country.

Graduating is a huge accomplishment for anyone, but it was especially admirable for someone like Floyd. Floyd grew up in poverty on the west side of Detroit. He watched his mother struggle to provide for him and his siblings. Graduating from Michigan State was truly a big deal for him. His life could've easily gone down a different path.

A few years ago, Floyd was unemployed. We talked a lot during that time. He'd call me before interviews, and we would talk through interview questions. I was happy to help him as he did for me when I was on the job market.

Floyd called me before a big interview with a well-established consulting firm. He was prepared and ready, as I knew he'd be. Afterward, he called me and said that he killed the interview and that he would hear back from the consulting firm soon. Floyd called me a week later. I was overjoyed to hear that he was offered the job! Six-figure salary, a quarterly bonus, and a flexible work schedule. The offer was perfect.

We celebrated! I was genuinely excited and happy for him. I knew that this was a huge step up in his career and that he was going to show his talent to the world.

A few days after our celebration, I called Floyd to check on him. He was quiet and seemed a bit somber. When I asked why, Floyd said that the company retracted the offer. I was shocked. He told me they found a post on his Facebook that they described as "distasteful."

I could tell that Floyd was devastated; I could hear the hurt in his voice. Just like that, his big opportunity was snatched away. I felt bad for him. He deserved the job. He deserved a big opportunity, but one silly Facebook post stopped him from getting there.

Floyd made that post roughly six years before he interviewed for the job. His post revolved around being willing to do anything to protect his family. It could have been interpreted as a threat. Someone within that company must've taken the time to screen Floyd's Facebook page.

So, I ask the question, was that post a reflection of who he is today? I don't think so. People grow and change. Obviously, I'm biased because Floyd and I are close, so I feel comfortable saying I know who he is.

Here's the thing though: The company he interviewed with didn't have that luxury. Floyd may have been a candidate for a great job, but he posted something that didn't align with what the company agrees with. They took his post at face value. They saw what they saw and judged him for it. In truth, they had every right to do so. The company Floyd interviewed with was a successful corporation. Corporations care deeply about their image and the people that represent them.

Whatever Floyd's post was, it didn't *represent* what that company sees as their image. On top of that, the company didn't owe Floyd anything. He wasn't one of their employees, he was simply a great candidate. In this instance, they saw something they didn't like and pulled the plug. No questions asked. No real explanation given.

This isn't an uncommon practice. According to CareerBuilder, a well-established job recruiting platform, the number of companies using social media to screen candidates has risen 59 percent in the past 15 years.

In 2017, 70 percent of the companies surveyed took time to look for job candidates on social media.

In addition, CareerBuilder listed the following as the top reasons for rejecting candidates based on their social media:

- Provocative or inappropriate content
- Drinking and drug use
- Discriminatory comments toward protected classes (race, religion, sex)

So, what's the moral of the story? People will not forgive you for the things you post online, especially if they are offended, uncomfortable, or upset because of it. Whether it be for a job interview or for a dinner date, people will judge you based on what you post on social media.

In some cases, what people think about your social media posts won't matter at all. They will judge you from thousands of miles away and you won't feel it one bit. You could post yourself half-naked, super drunk in Miami—some people will love it, some will like it, some will hate it. Regardless of what they feel, you may not be impacted by their feelings.

But here's the difference-maker: sometimes people's judgment can impact your life, even if you don't want it to.

Floyd and I learned a big lesson from this experience.

I'm proud to say that today Floyd is a well-respected regional manager for a very successful Fortune 500 company, a successful public speaker and mentor. He's a special guy with a unique story. Floyd isn't a completely different person from when he made that post, but he's more aware of how social media can affect his life's outcomes.

He has deleted a tweet or two to ensure the silly things he said at 20 years old don't come back to bite him a second time. Many can stand to learn from Floyd's experience.

3

PEOPLE WILL NOT FORGIVE YOU, PART 2

IN THE NOT-TOO-DISTANT PAST, I was a young, hot-tempered 15-year-old kid. At the time, I lived in Detroit but went to high school in Ferndale, a suburb of Detroit. For whatever reason, I developed a silly beef with one of my classmates. We'll call him Calvin. One day, Calvin and I decided that we were going to fight after school.

Originally, we were supposed to fight at the bus stop in Ferndale but ultimately decided to fight once we made it back to Detroit. Ferndale had a stable police presence at the time and neither one of us wanted to go to jail.

We rode the bus down Detroit's infamous Woodward Avenue. The tension grew as each stop brought us a bit closer to the location of our rumble. We exchanged glances every few stops; giving each other subtle cues that the fight was still on. We got off at 6 Mile and Woodward, which was roughly two miles from my home.

A few of our friends were on the bus. This made me nervous because I didn't want to lose a fight in front of my friends. The whole school would find out! Thankfully, this was a few years before people began pulling out their phones and screaming for blood as their camera flashes to record a brawl.

I got off the bus first, intentionally walking fast to ensure Calvin couldn't sneak up behind me. We exchanged words and Calvin began to step toward me. As soon as he was in range, I punched him as hard as I could. We fought like our lives were on the line.

From the street curb to the side of a building, we fought like hell. People drove by, honking their horns and screaming for us to stop. I remember wishing I had removed my book bag as I felt it slowing me down while we exchanged blows.

Eventually, one of our mutual friends broke up the fight. After it was over, Calvin and I briefly gabbed at each other before leaving.

I quickly walked home for fear of being arrested or jumped. Luckily, I wasn't arrested, and my school didn't find out about the incident.

In hindsight, what if someone recorded that fight? What if they held onto the video until I decided to go to college and then sent it to my school of choice? That university could decide that I wasn't a good fit for their program. They could, in some way, pressure me to disenroll from the university or retract my offer.

What if, years later, someone had sent that video to my job and it went viral? In some states, an employer could use the footage as grounds to fire me. They could say the video is a negative reflection of the company of their brand, beliefs, values, etc.

Both scenarios would have had major consequences on my life. But in this day and age, these aren't just made-up scenarios, they are realities for many.

In 2016, Mimi Groves, a young white woman, recorded herself saying the N-word on Snapchat. At the time of the recording, she was 15. One of her classmates, Jimmy Galligan, a black man, received the video from a friend three years later. For several reasons, Jimmy decided to hold on to the video. Both students spoke to the New York Times about their experiences.

According to the outlet, Jimmy posted the video online after Mimi announced publicly that she would be attending the University of Tennessee for undergrad.

The video was widely shared across multiple social media platforms. The fallout from the video and backlash from the university caused Mimi to withdraw from attending her dream school. Her dreams of cheerleading at the University of Tennessee were gone in a flash.

Both students attended Heritage High School in Leesburg, Virginia. Jimmy stated that he and other black students regularly experienced racism and unfair treatment.

He mentioned hearing his white classmates say the N-word and other hurtful racial slurs. When Jimmy brought these issues to school leadership, he didn't receive the support he expected.

In fact, a report titled "Systemic Equity Assessment: A Picture of Racial Equity Challenges and Opportunities in Loudoun County Public School District" stated that "despite efforts from the division, school site staff, specifically principals and teachers, indicate a low level of racial consciousness and racial literacy." This information was accompanied with other discouraging data points related to race relations within Heritage High School and its school district.

Ultimately, that post Mimi made when she was 15 had a huge impact on her life. There are many lessons to be learned here, but we'll focus on four:

1) THE INTERNET IS FOREVER. Let's state that one more time for the people in the back. The. Internet. Is. Forever. As of right now, anything you post will always "exist" in some fashion. Even if that post isn't available to you anymore, tweets, statuses, posts, and videos will remain out there in one way or another. They follow us quietly, regardless of if we decide to acknowledge them or not. If you really think about it, it's not hard to grasp.

At this point, we have the ability to screenshot and screen record anything we'd like. Nothing is stopping us from doing so. In an instant, you can take a photograph or record someone without their knowledge or consent. When we sign up for social media accounts, we agree to terms and conditions. In some cases, these terms and conditions allow our social media posts to be kept or archived, even if we delete them.

With this knowledge, we're given an opportunity to choose what we think is best for us. You have free will to make your own choices online, just remember that permanence exists.

2) SOMETIMES WE FAIL TO REALIZE HOW FAR THE THINGS WE SAY ONLINE CAN GO. For most people, typing up a rude sentence is much easier than saying it to someone's face, but even that can still come with consequences. Our words can travel farther than ever before. The internet has given us a near-infinite platform to say whatever we please. Every day, people get online and say things that have the potential to reach a worldwide audience. Sometimes those messages are good; other times the messages are terrible. Either way, our digital words have wings.

3) PEOPLE WILL NOT FORGIVE YOU FOR POOR CHOICES YOU'VE MADE, ESPECIALLY IF THOSE CHOICES FIND THEIR WAY ONLINE. The internet can be used as a platform for people to seek justice, and in some cases, revenge.

People generally do not care about the circumstances pertaining to other people's poor decision making.

Whether you're 15 or 55, people do not care, you're eligible for punishment for any poor decision that finds its way online. Today's social media culture fosters this behavior.

4) BEING ACCUSED IS ENOUGH. By enough, I mean that being accused of being something or someone that people do not think is *right* is enough ammunition to greatly impact your life, and that impact probably won't be in your favor. Notable athletes and celebrities have been subjected to this form of judgment.

For the purpose of illustrating my point, let's say another race of people existed. We'll refer to them as green people. Let's say you were accused of being an extreme racist toward green people, and these accusations gained a lot of attention on social media. Let's also say that you are a well-known business owner in your hometown, which is heavily populated by green people.

Putting aside the truth, if those accusations gained enough steam and people believed them to be real, there would be people online and in Real Life that would call for you to be *canceled*, unsupported, and everything in between. Some people would try to find out where you work, where you live, where your kids go to school, and more. People would call for your business to be closed and for you to deplatformed. This is a common practice in the US and beyond.

The impact would send shockwaves through your life. You could lose not only your business but relationships with friends and family, among other casualties. There's a chance you could find yourself on social media defending your morals and values in an effort to show the world you're not what people believe you to be.

Remember, this entire situation is based on you being perceived as a racist. It could be true, but it may not be. You haven't been convicted of a crime or sent to jail. You've simply been accused of being something that people do not think is *right*.

In this day and age, the truth can be hard to find and you don't have to be found guilty of a crime to have your life impacted. Understand that being accused of being a racist, sexist, misogynist, homophobe, fatphobe or anything else creates a unique opportunity for people online to *try to* ruin your life, regardless of if you are what they believe you to be or not. It doesn't mean they will be successful, but we know that they will try.

Today, guilt and accusation live in the same household. They are very close to each other, regardless of whether they should be.

Unless there is a monumental shift in our culture, this probably won't change.

To reflect on the situation between Mimi and Jimmy, I have a hard time deciding if I believe Jimmy's actions were *right* or not, but I do understand them.

He was mistreated and, from what I can tell, he wanted justice. I believe Jimmy wanted to see someone held accountable for their actions—a *change* from what he experienced in the past. I can't imagine how frustrated he may have been when he brought up racist incidents to school officials, only to see nothing happen. If I had to bet, Jimmy and other black students were likely tired of seeing white students continue to do the wrong thing without suffering any consequences.

At the same time, I can't imagine how devastated I would be if a choice I made at 15 years old impacted my future in such a devastating way.

I sometimes wonder, if potentially influential people in my life saw me fighting my classmate in the middle of 6 Mile Road, what would they think of me? If someone had recorded that incident, there is a chance I wouldn't be where I am today.

I could've gotten arrested. I could've lost out on the opportunities that afforded me the time, money, and freedom to write this book. The people driving by my fight could've seen me as a bad, uncivilized kid that belonged in jail instead of a respected university.

In the grand scheme of things, our personal opinions on Jimmy's actions really don't matter. We could debate all day on whether we think he was right or not. What ultimately matters is that we understand the way social media impacted this situation.

If you post something online, it will live forever.

There is, and always will be, a possibility that someone will use your own post against you in some way, shape, or fashion.

Our words travel far and if those words offend someone, there is a chance they will try to make you pay for what you said. In addition, being accused of being a bad person is *enough* to turn your life upside down, whether you are a bad person or not. Whether right or wrong, this is the reality we live in.

4

DELETE IT

WE ALL MAKE MISTAKES. Many of us, including myself, have posted something on the internet that we look back on and regret. You know, those pictures, tweets, and statuses that aren't in your best interest? Just like my friend Floyd, we've all done it. It happens. But as soon as you realize a post is not OK, you need to delete it.

Delete it. Delete this. Delete that. And delete that other thing, too. Some posts, without question, need to be deleted. Here are some posts that, without a doubt, need to be deleted.

1) ANYTHING THAT COULD IMPACT YOUR LIVELIHOOD OR FREEDOM: Don't think too hard about it. Just delete it. If your post could be used to indict you in a crime, delete it. If your job could use your post to fire you, delete it. Depending on what you do for a living, this may or may not be a big deal.

Employers may never come across your personal social media pages or they may not care, but if you have any inclination that you're risking your livelihood, just delete it. It's probably not worth the risk. It helps to keep this in mind *before* you post, too.

Think back to the past two chapters. We know that some employers look for job candidates on social media pages. We also know that universities can make decisions regarding enrollments due to what they see on social media. In theory, there's nothing stopping any other entity from doing the same.

2) ANYTHING THAT COULD IMPACT YOUR SAFETY OR THE SAFETY OF YOUR LOVED ONES: This tip is a no-brainer. Your safety is yours to care for. Trust me, it's not worth it. Do not provide people with your location or any information that could put you in danger.

The truth is, there are people online searching for this type of information to prey on others. From scammers to con artists, they're all out there and ready to steal from you, if not worse. Stay safe by keeping this information as private as possible.

Unfortunately, it's pretty easy to find people's personal info online. LifeLock, an identity protection company, recommends using Spokeo.com and Peoplefinders.com to see if your personal information is readily available online. I tried this.

I paid 99 cents on Spokeo.com and 95 cents on Peoplefinders.com and was able to find two previous addresses of mine, my current phone number, my birth month and birth year among other info. I was able to find friends' and family members' phone numbers, current addresses, previous addresses, email addresses, and more. All for less than two dollars.

On the bright side, Peoplefinders.com and Spokeo.com allow you to scrub your personal information from their website for free. In addition, LifeLock offers a variety of services to protect your personal information including credit monitoring and identity-theft protection.

3) ANYTHING THAT COULD HALT YOUR GOALS, DREAMS, AND ASPIRATIONS: Some posts fall into a bucket that's a bit harder to measure. They may not stop you from making money or from living safely, but they could stop you from getting to where you want to go in life.

If there is anything on your social media pages that could halt your goals, dreams, and aspirations, delete it. Your dreams are big and important! Put your future first and delete anything that could harm it.

I say all this to say, I have friends that are much different than me. They do and say whatever they want online and that's a good route for them to be happy with their lives. Social media culture encourages us to be open, and many people enjoy that benefit.

Just remember this: before posting something that could impact your livelihood, safety, or future, think about what you have to lose. We all have something to lose—relationships with family, job opportunities, credibility with friends. Some of us may feel this more than others, but the internet doesn't have to be an open diary, especially if you have something to protect.

There are people in your life that want to see you financially stable. They want to celebrate birthdays and holidays with you, and of course, they want to see you achieve your wildest dreams. Let's keep it that way.

In general, deleting old posts actually makes a lot of sense. People grow and change. Your old posts may not be derogatory or ignorant, but they may just no longer reflect who you are.

If this is the case, it makes sense for you to distance yourself from things you said in the past, especially if those things don't match who you've become or who you aspire to be.

Lastly, I once saw someone tweet that they hate Beyoncé. Hands down, one of the wildest tweets out there! At first, I was confused how someone could feel that way. Second, I wondered if that person knew anything about the Beyhive and their relentless protection of their queen.

Nevertheless, that was a crazy tweet. That's a wild thing to say online. Even if you did feel that way, which is hard to imagine, delete that before someone sees it.

5

ALGORITHMS & U

HAVE you ever watched one of those scary movies, where the monsters can't see, but their other senses (hearing, smell) are so good that they don't need to be able to see to find the unlucky humans? These films typically follow a few protagonists. These heroes watch in horror as other characters meet their end to the blind, but very deadly monsters.

In these movies the monsters can't *see*, but they don't need to be able to see to be a threat to our heroes. They have other tools that make them extremely dangerous.

In a funny way, social media algorithms are the same. The algorithms used on the popular apps like TikTok and Twitter are very, very good at learning information about us. They don't necessarily need to read our text messages or listen to our phone conversations to figure out our interests.

You may be wondering, what is an algorithm? According to Merriam Webster, an algorithm is a step-by-step procedure for solving a problem or accomplishing some end. Regarding social media, algorithms are used to figure out what you're interested in; they are used to categorize your interest and keep you engaged by directing you to the content that lines up with those interests.

In mid-2021, the Wall Street Journal took time to study TIkTok's algorithm. They created multiple "bot" accounts with different interests to understand how the algorithm works. They came back with some really awesome findings! They found that the algorithm can figure out the user's interest within two hours or less. Soon after, the fake user accounts saw a steady stream of content that matched their interests.

The Wall Street Journal noted that the content being fed to users is tightly tailored to the user's preferences. If the user gravitates towards depressing content, TikTok will place that content on their timeline. If the user gravitates towards funny content, once again, TikTok will place that content on their timeline.

So, what do we do with this information? This info gives insight into how algorithms are able to help these companies become big, influential, billion-dollar businesses. We must understand that the popular social media platforms wouldn't be in those positions if they weren't aggressive in the way they acquire, interpret, and apply information, data and metrics.

TikTok is aggressive in their approach to discovering what we like, feeding us that content, and using our engagement to make money. This is a winning formula for TikTok, and their CEO, Zhang Yiming, whose estimated worth exceeds $40 billion!

At its core, the algorithm is a tool used for the company's benefit. Its job isn't to monitor your mental health as you scroll the app.

That's your job. It's on us to understand and monitor the content being fed to us.

You may wonder why you consistently see certain types of content on your timeline. More than likely, it's because you're constantly interacting with that content. You're probably not scrolling past it quickly. More than likely, you're liking it, viewing it, opening it up and in other ways showing the algorithm that you're interested in that content.

Now, you may truly enjoy the flow of your timeline. You may not feel a need to change anything, but if you are someone who is being inundated with content that doesn't suit you, try to change it up. Try to interact with that content less. If you're able, use the apps tools to note that you aren't interested in that content. It's within your power to disengage from that content so that you create a better and potentially healthier experience.

Understand that if we're not paying attention, algorithms have the ability to know more about us and our interests than we do.

Before this book was published, I was asked about today's social media apps having the ability to read our minds. A friend asked, "Do they read our text messages and listen-in on our phone calls?" My answer is this:

THEY DON'T HAVE TO. We use the apps consistently and give them ample opportunities to learn a lot of information about us. We agree to the Terms of Service laid out by each app. We agree to be marketed to and studied. With this being the case, we're offering up more than enough info for them to create an engaging user experience that can generate profit.

Today's popular social media apps are just like the monsters in those scary movies. They can't *see* everything, but they have other "senses" that make them very deadly.

6

CANCEL CULTURE

In 2005, Kanye West dropped his second album, "Late Registration." Each song gave me a different feeling. From "Roses" to "Gold Digger," it was a complete body of work—a masterpiece from Chicago's native son. It was clear that Kanye West was a maestro; a special talent that deserved praise.

I was a high school freshman at that time. Eager to chase girls and get into trouble, I would steal my mom's truck to drive around Detroit's west side. Because I was young and without a license, I didn't speed. I would cruise and listen to music. I ruffled through the truck's center console searching for the right CD to match my mood. I often picked "Late Registration."

I always played "Drive Slow." The beat was amazing. The production was crazy! Paul Wall slowly crept on to the track, bringing that unique, Houston flavor to the song. It was the perfect song for me—a kid that wanted to feel cool and not go to jail for driving illegally!

Fast forward to 2013. Kanye was still one of my favorite artists, but I began to see him in a different light. He named his sixth album "Yeezus" (a play on Jesus), which I thought was odd. Tracks like "I Am a God" made me a tad bit uncomfortable. I thought, *This guy is putting himself next to God. That's a little weird.*

Oddly enough, I was never bothered whenever Jay-Z called himself Hov or Hova (short for Jehovah or God). In my lifetime, I can't remember ever hearing anyone question it.

In fact, I catch myself calling Jay-Z "Hov" from time to time. Especially when I argue with friends about who is the best rapper of all time. I'm quick to say, "Hov!"

By the time 2018 rolled around, I found myself listening to Kanye less and less.

Midway into that year, Kanye drew headlines over comments he made during a visit with the TMZ staff in Los Angeles. During the conversation he stated, "When you hear about slavery for 400 years… For 400 years? That sounds like a choice," during his visit, in reference to the centuries of enslavement black people endured in America.

I was deeply offended by Kanye's comments for more than one reason. I'm extremely confident that my ancestors didn't "choose" to be slaves. Also, I found his comments to be ignorant and insensitive to the atrocities enslaved people faced in America and beyond. His comments disgusted me.

Many people shared my sentiments; some wrote articles and made posts on their feelings toward Kanye. There was no way around it, Kanye was wrong.

At that moment I decided that Kanye was "canceled." You've probably heard this term before, but let's define it before moving on.

According to Dictonary.com,

> *Cancel culture* refers to the popular practice of withdrawing support for (*canceling*) public figures and companies after they have done or said something considered objectionable or offensive. *Cancel culture* is generally discussed as being performed on social media in the form of group shaming.

So, what does it mean to "cancel" someone?

According to Merriam Webster,

> "To cancel someone (usually a celebrity or other well-known figure) means to stop giving support to that person. The act of canceling could entail boycotting an actor's movies or no longer reading or promoting a writer's works.
>
> The reason for cancellation can vary, but it usually is due to the person in question having expressed an objectionable opinion or having conducted themselves in a way that is unacceptable, so that continuing to patronize that person's work leaves a bitter taste."

I think these definitions hit the nail on the head. The only thing I would add is that some people encourage others to *cancel* people as well. The "group shaming" piece of cancel culture has a wide-ranging impact. People rally support to *cancel* everything from businesses, shows, music, and of course, other people.

To bring it back to Kanye, since he was canceled for me, I could no longer listen to his music or support him in any shape or form.

Though I was interested, I ultimately decided not to listen to his ninth album, "Jesus is King." Between his slavery comments and his odd Twitter rants, I was done. I was vocal with friends and family about my feelings on Kanye and whatever I felt his "problem" was.

My reasoning for being upset with Kanye felt legitimate then and they still feel legitimate today. He said something I really didn't agree with, and I couldn't bring myself to let it go, but I did wonder if I was being judgmental.

I wondered if refusing to forgive one of my heroes made sense. Honestly, I wondered if I thought I was better or smarter than he was. I've made mistakes too, and I've said things I shouldn't have as well.

So, I ask the question: What if everyone refused to forgive people because of one thing they said? What if everyone refused to forgive people because of one mistake they made?

Let me give a scenario: Kanye West opens a music school in inner-city Chicago aimed at teaching the arts to minorities.

The music school is free to the students and provides them with a unique opportunity to learn and develop their talent. Students leave Kanye's school with great careers and opportunities to make an impact on the world through their art and music. Would I still see Kanye as a bad person because of something he said in 2018, or would I see him as something else?

Here lies one of the core flaws in cancel culture: Human beings have the ability to do the right thing and the wrong thing within the same minute. Humans are beautiful but flawed. We can grow, change, learn, and do good even though we've done bad.

One minute, I could refuse to help my mother carry heavy groceries into her home. In the next minute, I could send my little brother money to buy a textbook for his college classes.

One scenario makes me sound like an uncaring son while the other makes me sound like a thoughtful brother. In truth, I could be both. I'm human.

In 2019, former President Barack Obama spoke at the Obama Foundation Summit. President Obama gave his opinion on some of the behaviors he's observed on social media. Obama stated "The world is messy. There are ambiguities. People who do really good stuff have flaws," he told the audience.

His message was a simple one that has been repeated throughout history. "The line dividing good and evil cuts through the heart of every human being," Russian philosopher Alexandr Solzhenitsyn once said.

Cancel culture asks us to judge people. At times, it asks us to throw people away because of the choices they've made. Don't get me wrong, there are people in the world who have done terrible things and no longer deserve support or praise.

Some people absolutely need to be called out for their wrongs. No one is above criticism. At times, people must face consequences for the things they say and do.

However, we should try to help people before throwing them away. When able, we should try to educate them before destroying them. I'm thankful to have close friends who I trust to have intimate conversations. We talk about everything from politics to relationships, and most recently, sexuality.

Some of my friends were able to teach me a new perspective. At times, I was defensive of my opinion, but ultimately, I grew to be appreciative of the criticism.

In hindsight, I needed the criticism; it helped me grow. I've grown to appreciate people that decide to spend their time and energy to help me become a better human being. In a perfect world, we would extend this same courtesy to everyone.

Social media gives us the power to do so, but we often throw stones from afar instead of offering knowledge or assistance. We can act as a virtual judge and jury, or we can decide to teach instead.

I haven't listened to Kanye's most recent albums, but I do own a pair of Yeezys. If Kanye produces something for Pusha T or Big Sean, I'm going to listen to it. So, did I actually cancel him? Or am I a hypocrite?

It is hard to say. But what I have learned is that I have flaws, just like everyone else. I shouldn't be so quick to judge others.

Kanye West is a talented man and like each of us, he has the ability to influence the world in a positive way if he chooses. Remember, we all have the ability to do great things and help many people, all while making mistakes, offending others, and having hiccups along the way.

Here's this chapter's takeaway. You'll see the Greater Than (>) symbol used a few times throughout this book.

1. Educating > Cancelling
2. Helping > Cancelling
3. At times, Cancelling is valid

7

SEEKING HAPPINESS ONLINE

ON THE EARLY morning of Thursday, May 28th, 2020, I got a call from my father. His call came through at about 6am that day. My dad and I typically talk in the evening, so I knew something wasn't right. He was somber, but straight to the point. My older sister, Ewanda, had died in a car accident.

This was devastating news. My sister was kind of like my first superhero. She taught me life lessons through her actions and always found a way to save me when I was in trouble. When I was in high school, she would pay me to run errands for her.

She could've easily done these things on her own, but I think she wanted an excuse to give me money and speak to me about my future.

Before I saw my potential, she saw it. She made me a better person and I miss her deeply. I miss visiting her to talk about my goals and dreams. When she passed, I was broken, and I knew it.

Like many other families, 2020 hit my family hard. Earlier that year, I lost my stepfather and my aunt. Not long after losing my stepfather, I lost my job due to the COVID-19 pandemic. Like many others, I questioned how I was going to make ends meet.

At that time, I was in a very emotional space. The night before my sister's funeral, I went to the bar. Yes, in the middle of a pandemic, I went out in the heart of Atlanta to drink with my friends. That decision probably sits on my Mount Rushmore of poor choices.

I was sad and afraid. I didn't know if I had the courage to deal with what was in front of me. I was going home to come face-to-face with the truth. My sister was gone.

The next day, a mostly sober Tyler Hendon flew to Detroit to say farewell to his big sister.

Her homegoing was beautiful. My family, adorned in dresses and suits, gathered on Detroit's riverfront to say goodbye. The day was bittersweet, but I'm very thankful that we were able to come together for my superhero.

After my sister's funeral, I did something that I later thought was very odd. I posted a picture of myself to Instagram. I took the photo the night before in Atlanta. Black glasses, a black shirt, black ripped jeans, and black Converse shoes. I looked good! Or at least, I wanted to *feel* that way.

In hindsight, what I was trying to do by posting the picture is clear. I wanted to appear as if I was OK. I wanted to look like I was still strong. As if I wasn't hurting, badly. And, above anything else, I wanted to feel happiness during a dark time in my life.

I posted my picture and kept my eyes on the notifications. Vigilantly, I watched as the likes grew. Each like, each little comment, I soaked in. I wanted to feel good. I didn't realize it, but I was trying to use the "likes" as a pick-me-up.

Why did I make that choice?

Adam Alter, a very successful author, and professor is the writer of two New York Times best-selling books, *Irresistible* and *Drunk Tank Pink*. Alter has received wide recognition for his work on technology addiction. In 2017, Alter spoke with Business Insider regarding his work. Alter compared getting a "like" on Instagram to the experience humans feel when drinking alcohol or smoking a cigarette.

> "The minute you take a drug, drink alcohol, smoke a cigarette, if those are your poison, when you get a like on social media, all of those experiences produce dopamine, which is a chemical that is associated with pleasure," he said.

> "When someone likes an Instagram post or any content you share, it's a little bit like taking a drug. As far as your brain is concerned it's a very similar experience."

What is dopamine? Dopamine is a chemical that naturally occurs in our bodies. It works as a neurotransmitter, and as Alter mentioned, it plays a role in how we feel pleasure. Drugs like cocaine can supercharge the dopamine within our bodies, giving us a high that temporarily makes us feel amazing.

Knowing this, would it be far-fetched to say I wanted to experience the "high" of getting likes on my post? Not at all. At that moment, I wanted to feel happy so maybe, for a few minutes, I felt normal. Somehow, someway, I felt this would be the best avenue for me to feel some sort of satisfaction during a very difficult time in my life.

The truth is this behavior is dangerous, but not abnormal. Some of us are susceptible to chasing what I like to call a "Likes High."

A Likes High can be defined as a temporary sense of joy or accomplishment due to the perceived success of a social media post. Whether it be an Instagram photo, Facebook post, or TikTok video, all these platforms create an avenue for us to chase a Likes High.

In the Social Dilemma, a well-crafted documentary that focuses on consequences of social media's growth, Dr. Anna Lembke stated "So here's the thing: social media is a drug and we have a basic biological imperative to connect with other people." Dr. Lembke went on to say "There's no doubt that a vehicle like social media, that optimizes this connection between people, is going to have the potential for addiction."

So, I ask the question, have you ever posted something and felt some type of buzz or high because of its success? How did you feel once you deemed the post successful? Take a minute or two to think about it. Feel free to note what you felt here:

_____

_____

_____

_____

_____

_____

On the opposite end, what if the post is unsuccessful? Have you ever posted something that you thought you would receive a lot of likes or validation, but it didn't? How did you feel then? Take some time to reflect on that experience.

Many of us have experienced these emotions. Joy when we receive the attention we were looking for, and disappointment when a post doesn't get the attention or validation we expected.

Chasing any kind of high can be dangerous, especially when it involves something you're addicted to or engage in as regularly as social media. We all know people that are chasing these highs—we may even be those people! In my experience, people chasing highs can become desperate and vulnerable.

They are more likely to do things out of their character to reach that high. Their judgment can become skewed as well as their ability to determine a good choice from a bad one.

Have you ever seen someone post something on social media that you thought was odd or cringeworthy? If you spend a fair amount of time on social media, I can almost guarantee you have seen *or* done this.

Comparing social media use to a drug like cocaine may seem like a stretch, but both can be dangerously addictive and impact our state of mind. Both give us an opportunity to chase a high.

We need to be very, very careful about the way we allow addictive social media to bring us up, bring us down, and how we interpret those experiences in our Real Life.

In addition, we must understand that people don't really care about our social media accounts, they care about *their* social media accounts. This is a key piece in understanding why social media validation is tricky. I'll explain. Dr. Mike Brooks, a licensed psychologist and author, examined this in 2019. In a blog titled "Proof That No One Really Cares About Our Social Media Posts," Brooks asked several interesting questions. A few are listed below:

1. "Try to think of a specific social media post of someone else's that you "liked" last week. Go ahead. I'll wait right here. Keep thinking...wait for it...got one? How long did it take you to come up with one? Were you even able to?"

2. "If you were able to recall someone's post from last week that you "liked," how much time did you spend thinking about their post *after* liking it? My guess is, none."

Through this unique test, Brooks concluded that many people struggle to remember a social media post they liked last week, if they can remember at all. In addition, he states that social validation is enjoyable, but not nourishing.

His argument is quite strong. No one really cares about your posts because they are too consumed with *their* posts.

Many of us are too caught up with the look, feel, and position of our social media to really care about how everyone else is *performing*.

Your social media pages may be appealing, eye-catching, or noteworthy, but more than likely it isn't other people's concern when they start and end their day.

Now, there is nothing wrong with enjoying social media. Ideally, we should enjoy the many apps that connect us to the world. Connecting with friends, family and your interests is a good thing! We just have to make sure to do it in a healthy way.

To do this, we must refrain from connecting our happiness to likes, a.k.a., validation. We must foster and maintain a sense of self-love and peace regardless of what people in our comments tell us or how many followers we have.

Remember, seeking validation from other people online will never be fulfilling. It will never be *truly* satisfying. There will always be some type of void. There will always *seem* to be something more to achieve, even if that something is unattainable and unworthy of your time.

8

BE KIND TO YOURSELF

READ the title of this chapter again. I'll wait.

…..Done? In today's world, it can be very, *very* difficult to be kind to yourself. Here's why.

Have you ever looked at your timeline and saw a lot of winners? New cars, fancy degrees, big houses, new relationships, fun vacations, classy weddings, great bodies, perfect marriages, beautiful children and many, many other things that look GOOD online.

At times, our timeline can be like looking into a *Mirage*. People's lives look awesome on the outside looking in, but all may not be as it seems. Many of my peers, the cool people known as millennials, are quick to post the positive things happening in our lives.

And why wouldn't we, right? Most people don't want to post their pain and anguish online.

In 2020 and 2021, a lot of us found ourselves posting pictures of the family and friends we lost due to the pandemic and other unexpected circumstances. We mourned them in our statuses and asked for prayers for our families.

I feel comfortable saying that experience wasn't a joyful one for us. We would much rather post the positive moments in our lives and allow them to overshadow the negative ones.

Many of us put our accomplishments on full display and we should, we deserve to, but it can be hard to watch your friends' highlight reels flash across your timeline when you're going through tough times in your life. When you're down, your timeline may feel like cleaning the floor after an award ceremony. Everyone's happy and looks stunning but you're only there to clean the auditorium after they celebrate.

I worked for Amazon for roughly three and a half years. During that time, I was promoted into a position that paid very well. At the time, I was deeply connected to my work. Every day that I walked into work, I felt needed. I worked hard and felt important. In my last year at Amazon, my relationship with my manager went sour unexpectedly and it led to my leaving the company.

For about a year I searched high and low for jobs. I had little luck and eventually had to take temporary jobs to make ends meet. I bounced from temp agency to temp agency, hoping to find something that would stick. I went from making a six-figure salary to working odd jobs for $9.75 an hour.

By the time I found a solid job, I had to sell off virtually every investment I had to ensure I was able to pay my bills. Some of those investments included Amazon stock, which has grown in value greatly since I sold it. A humbling experience to say the least.

So, here's my question to you: Do you think I told the world I was going broke? Do you think I tweeted or posted a story about how I was running out of money? Or that I had to work a double shift to pay my light bill?

I most certainly did not. As far as the world knew, everything was fine with me. To be honest, I barely told my friends.

I didn't post online about losing my job. I didn't tell the world that I was struggling to find a job and that my Real Life felt like it was in shambles, but I guarantee you I felt it every single day. This brings us to the main point of this chapter:

Be kind to yourself. Everyone's life may look awesome on social media, but keep in mind that may not be the case. This is one of the big factors that makes social media a *Mirage*. Some people post their pain and problems online, but many do not.

Many of us would rather face our challenges quietly rather than telling our followers that we are struggling.

Our timelines are often filled with highlights that reflect what we want the world to see, which may not be an accurate reflection of what we're experiencing at the moment.

Beginning today, Stop comparing your Real Life to what you see on the internet. You're not doing yourself any favors. In fact, you're actually hurting yourself. Adam Alter, who is clearly my favorite author on this topic, stated that seeing the best version of everyone else's life makes you feel deprived; meaning that this experience could make you feel down or unsatisfied. I agree with him fully. If you compare your Real Life to everyone else's highlight reel on social media, you'll never be happy.

In my case, I had to stop comparing myself to people with master's degrees, MBAs and PHDs. Around graduation season, which is

May and December in the US, I would love to see my friends in their caps and gowns as they walk the stage to receive their well-earned degrees. They look amazing leveling up!

But at the same time, I would look in the mirror and wonder why I wasn't in that position. At times, I would question why my test scores weren't good enough for my dream schools. I saw the accomplishments of my friends, took a deep breath and felt like I was unsuccessful.

In today's social media era, comparing your life to others is a very easy thing to do and this comparison occurs naturally because social media is an impactful tool in the way we stay connected and make relationships.

You don't have to push yourself to make the comparison; they are right in front of you to do with what you please. This is especially true if you use social media on a daily basis.

Is there any area of your life that you compare to what you see from others on social media? Be honest with yourself. Take a minute or two to think about it and write it down here.

_____

_____

_____

_____

_____

_____

Done? Kudos to you for acknowledging what I like to call the "Area of Comparison." If you want to offer yourself some grace, accept and acknowledge that these comparisons can impact your mental well-being. Remember, this Area of Comparison looks different for everyone.

Due to algorithms, what you see online may look completely different from what others see.

Maybe it's the careers or businesses you see that *seem* phenomenal. You know, those opportunities that give you an important title like M.D., CEO, or PhD. Many of us strive to be in important positions and want to feel successful, but we forget that life isn't perfect for the people that have accomplished what we strive to become.

Social media does not accurately depict the struggles of people across the US who are overworked and under pressure, regardless of their job title. Many doctors work an exorbitant number of hours and only about half of small businesses last five years.

Now, please don't take this as a deterrent for pursuing your dreams but understand that your next step will come with challenges just like your last one did.

You may not be super career driven. Your area of comparison could be different.

Maybe it's the relationships you see that *seem* perfect. You know, those relationships that people see as *goals*. Around the holidays, we all see couples in their comfy pajamas taking beautiful pictures near the Christmas tree perfectly positioned by the fireplace. Their stockings are hung, and everyone looks happy. What an amazing couple and a picture-perfect snapshot of their life, right?

In truth, they could be miserable. They could be going through a rough patch in their relationship. They may have argued and fought minutes, perhaps even seconds, before that photo was taken. Or they could be madly in love! They could be enjoying every moment together. They could be having the best holiday season of their lives. Unless you know these people in Real Life there's no way to really know what the truth is. So, if you see these beautiful couples on Instagram, just double tap the picture and keep scrolling.

If there was ever a time to stop comparing yourself to other people, it's now. Since the rise of COVID-19, 4 million people and counting have lost their lives due to this terrible virus. Their families rocked and communities burdened with grief due to these unexpected losses. In November 2020, the U.S. Census Bureau reported that 83 million American adults said they experienced some level of difficulty paying for everyday expenses like food, rent, and car payments.

In fact, these hardships are even greater among households with children. Black and Latino Americans were among the highest number of households experiencing financial hardship. Food and housing insecurity has sharply increased.

Understand that all around the world, people are suffering in more ways than one and social media doesn't always reflect that. Be thankful for what you have and end the comparisons.

You never know what someone else is going through, even if they did just post a picture partying it up and drinking 1942 Tequila on a boat in Tulum.

Adults must realize that our youth are more susceptible to these comparisons that we ever were.

If we're paying attention, it's easy to see this change. Adult women of today did not grow up with this level of pressure to have a great body. Business Insider examined the rise in Brazilian butt lifts, also known as "BBLs." According to the American Society for Aesthetic Plastic Surgery, "BBLs" increased by 90.3% between 2015 to 2019.

In addition, there has been an increase in young women pursuing these types of cosmetic procedures.

An uptick in young women pursuing cosmetic procedures is a reflection of our culture, and if we think for one minute that social media isn't impacting this rise, we're lying to ourselves.

Our youth are surrounded by screens that can bombard them with unfair comparisons, half-truths, falsehoods and inundate them with information. Those factors create pressure to *be* and *have* things that they may not need.

If you were over the age of 25 by 2020, I guarantee you did not have this level of access to the world when you were a child. I fear that the harder it becomes to see the truth, the scarier the world will be for young people. Adults have a major responsibility to educate them as best we can on the experiences they'll have online and how to interpret those experiences.

To the youth of the world, please understand there are a lot of falsehoods out there and you must do your best to determine what's true and what isn't. Please do not place your Real Life up against the online lives of others. If you do this, you risk creating unfair comparisons between yourself and online personas.

Whether it be people's lives, how much money they have, what they do for a living, what kind of cars they own, it may all be a facade. Some of it is real, some of it isn't. Either way, you need to be careful buying into social media culture.

Lastly, please be kind to yourself.

9

INFLUENCE DOES NOT EQUAL LEADERSHIP

IN 2005, Lil Wayne released "The Carter 2," his fifth studio album. It was and is still, to this day, one of the best albums I've ever heard. My close friends and I kept it in rotation. We would debate over which songs were the best. I liked "Fireman" and "Best Rapper Alive." Our favorite rapper, "Wayne," was untouchable. We dressed like him and watched all his music videos on BET. Some of my cousins and friends even got tattoos modeled after his.

Lil Wayne was influential way before social media truly popped! He was an icon to us and in many ways, still is. Over the course of two decades, he's found a way to remain an influential figure in music and culture.

In recent years, Lil Wayne has made several statements on racism in America. He's said he doesn't feel connected to the Black Lives Matter movement and that his life was saved by a white police officer, which had a huge impact on his views on racism.

He stated that he hasn't experienced racism and seemed to struggle to acknowledge it even exists.

In late 2020, Lil Wayne took a photo alongside former President Donald Trump, in what could be interpreted as a show of support for Trump's then-reelection campaign. Lil Wayne posted the photo to his Instagram and Twitter; in the photo he smiled and gave a thumbs up alongside the soon-to-be-former president.

One could argue that, once again, Lil Wayne showed that his beliefs didn't align with that of Black Lives Matter protesters or social justice advocates who adamantly fought against Trump's actions and rhetoric.

In this instance, Lil Wayne can be seen as an example of a highly influential individual that comes from a marginalized community but should not be seen as a spokesperson for that community.

In his case, influence does not equal leadership. He will always be an icon, but probably won't ever be seen as a voice for important issues in America and beyond. In fairness, I doubt he even wants to be.

Social media has made it harder to distinguish between who is a leader and who is not. A person with a massive platform or millions of followers can quickly be seen as a leader, even if they don't want to be perceived that way.

I saw a post on Instagram that read "Rappers are not the leaders of black people." From my perspective, that quote doesn't mean an artist, celebrity, or influential person cannot be a community leader —*it simply means that having a voice, fame, or position of power does NOT automatically make you a leader.*

There is a very, very fine line between the two concepts, but to understand the world we live in, we must realize the importance of separating influence and popularity from leadership.

Artists and celebrities can definitely be leaders, if they choose to be. G Herbo, a well-known artist from Chicago, is a leader. In September 2020, he purchased his former elementary school in an effort to turn it into a youth center. He also spearheaded a mental-health program aimed to aid underprivileged communities. He has been very vocal about the traumatic experiences he endured growing up in Chicago.

G Herbo has used his Instagram account, which has nearly 7 million followers, to spread information on free mental-health resources.

He has encouraged people to seek help for their problems, while staying true to his Chi-town roots; his lyrics are still raw and true while his community work shows that he is in tune with the struggles that burden many members of Chicago's youth.

G Herbo is a strong example of leadership for several reasons. Leadership requires knowledge, experience, and, above all, the ability to work on behalf of that cause. G Herbo understands the tough situations people deal with in inner-city Chicago, he's dealt with and received counselling for his own trauma, and he's shown that he's willing to work on behalf of the causes he believes in.

Nipsey Hussle is another example of a highly influential artist that's also a leader. The well-respected rapper and entrepreneur invested heavily into his South Los Angeles community and beyond. In 2013, Nipsey quickly sold 1,000 physical copies of his mixtape, "Crenshaw", for $100 a piece; a brave, brilliant move that encouraged his supporters to buy into his success.

In 2018, Nipsey and his business partners at PUMA revitalized basketball courts and donated $10,000 to 59th Street Elementary School, in the neighborhood Nipsey grew up in. According to CBS News, the day before Nipsey's death in 2019, he was planning to meet with LAPD leadership to address gun violence among the youth in Los Angeles. I could go on and on about his community work and genius as a businessman.

Nipsey's Instagram account, which still stands as tall as he is, is filled with images of his work, influence, and leadership. If you scroll back far enough, you'll find a photo of Nipsey signing red album booklets for *Crenshaw*. This is my favorite picture of him. To me, it symbolizes his strong belief in himself and how he was willing to take a chance on that belief.

Nipsey was in tune with street life but also in tune with his purpose, his people and The Marathon that drove him to become a two-time Grammy-winning artist.

Through his music and activism, he impacted his community and became a face for self-belief. In his death, he inspired and united people.

Last time that I checked, that's the kind of impact leaders make.

Their actions and words outlive them. Leaders like Nipsey have the ability to create strong, blue waves that don't die out. Even though Nipsey is no longer present in the flesh, his success and impact are still felt today.

Social media doesn't create leaders like Nipsey Hussle and G Herbo. They create themselves through their experiences and willingness to help others.

To bring it back to Lil Wayne, he's used his voice and influence in a different fashion. He doesn't have to stand for important causes, as that may not be who he is or align with his interest, but to consider him a voice for marginalized communities would be irresponsible and unfair to him and to the people that work every day on behalf of those communities.

That doesn't mean Lil Wayne hasn't helped these communities in one way or another. He has given back to his community in New Orleans and beyond. However, Wayne does not occupy the same space as someone like G Herbo or Nipsey Hussle when it comes to cementing themselves as a leader even though he is very popular and influential.

Remember this:

1. People can exist in the same space but serve different purposes in that space.
2. We must be able to discern who is actually a leader and why.

Here's a fictional example:

Let's say that ESSENCE is planning for their highly anticipated yearly gathering, ESSENCE Festival.

The festival's key topic in our exercise revolves around the physical and mental health of black Americans.

The festival's planning board decides to invite intelligent, talented black health advocates from around the world to participate in the event. In this scenario, Kerry Washington, a very successful actress, producer, and director, is chosen to be the keynote speaker for the festival's final seminar.

In the past, Washington has tweeted about her concerns for the health of black Americans and their mental and physical well-being. She has a massive platform on social media because of her celebrity status. She's gained many followers due to her ability to reach many people through social media.

With this being the case, is she truly the best person to speak at the seminar *or* is her platform the biggest? It depends. There is a chance that she could lack the knowledge, experience and work history needed to lead this big conversation in front of 500,000 festival attendees.

She may be a strong advocate for these issues, but she also may not have worked in this field or done the needed research to be an expert.

Or she could be the perfect person for the seminar! She could have received multiple degrees from well-respected institutions, certifying her as an expert in the field. She could have spent years of her life working with black people with physical and mental-health issues.

If this is the case, it makes sense for her to lead this conversation. In this scenario, she's shown that she has the knowledge, experience, and ability to make an impact in this space.

It can be difficult to discern, but we must do better at spotting the difference between someone with a ton of followers and someone who is using their influence as a leader. Social media constantly blurs these lines.

We must do our best to cut through the noise and make sound decisions about who we should follow and trust.

To summarize, here are two, simple equations on influence and leadership. Remember, (>) means Greater than and (=) means Equals.

1. Knowledge, Experience, and ability to Work = Best/Leader
2. Knowledge, Experience, and ability to Work is > Most Well-Known

You can be the most well-known *and* the best, but they are not always a pair.

10

THE HOOK

HAVE you ever been in a social setting where people barely talked? Instead, they just looked at their phones? Or maybe they looked at their phones, "people watched," and made minimum conversation? Many of us have experienced this. These types of anti-social interactions aren't uncommon in our society.

Now, this doesn't mean we are becoming less skilled at interacting with other humans, in-person. What it simply means is that we now have more opportunities to "tune out" of whatever is going on around us and connect to the online world via our devices.

This is not totally the fault of social media, but it has played a part.

Before we can understand why we see an increase in people being antisocial in social settings, we must first understand why we're hooked on social media in the first place. There are multiple factors, but we'll focus on a few. Outside of interacting with friends and family online, we also enjoy the fact that our favorite social media apps typically have more than one function.

This is in part due to the creators and engineers of the apps understanding this:

Time is Money.

The more time you spend on the app, the more money they are able to make. Social media apps benefit from your time spent on the apps because it allows them an opportunity to sell ads and "monetize" the experience in any way possible.

Monetize simply means to turn something into money. In this instance, the creators and engineers want to find ways to turn your engagement and membership into cash.

Think about it like this: if you owned a zoo, would you only have lions in it? Probably not. To attract a crowd, you'd probably want the zoo to be diverse. You would definitely want lions (everyone loves lions) but you'd also want elephants, monkeys, tigers, rhinos, giraffes, and other animals that people love. You would sell snacks like popcorn, ice cream, and pizza to make additional profit. If you were really profit driven, you would charge people to park and find little ways to make an extra buck or two.

Today's popular social media apps are like a zoo. The experts at these platforms want you to have options. They want you to interact with their platform in more ways than one to ensure you're active, engaged, and ready to return for more. These experts understand that companies will pay millions to market to their users.

The experience may be free, but we *pay* for the apps by agreeing to be marketed to and exposed to consistent opportunities for the businesses to make cash.

The app developers have unique ways of sneaking ads into the universe of experiences we have when logged on. The things being marketed to you may not feel forced; oftentimes, they feel like a normal part of the experience. TikTok is great at this. They have resources and tips for anyone willing to jump into the ad space. On their website, TikTok states "Don't Make Ads. Make a Connection." "Don't Make Ads. Make a New Trend." "Don't Make Ads. Make TikToks."

There is a science to this. If you did plan to advertise, TikTok wants those ads to be engaging, organic content that users enjoy.

In addition, this impact plays a part in social media apps adding new features. They want you hooked.

New features create opportunities for increased engagement, which the apps can use for further monetization.

Remember, the popular social media apps are profit driven companies. They understand the power of keeping you engaged, and they know far too well that time is money.

Take Facebook for instance. Without thinking too hard, can you name four different things you can do on Facebook? Take your time to think of four. Jot them down below. If you aren't a Facebook user, use your favorite social media app instead.

_____

_____

_____

_____

_____

_____

Done? On Facebook you can post statuses, message friends, like friends' photos, promote a business, start or join a club, online date, shop, play games, find jobs, read the news, and more.

I can guarantee that if Facebook only allowed people to post statuses it wouldn't be as popular as it is today. The smart people at Facebook have created a universe of experiences for their users. In theory, Facebook could argue that their platform has something for everyone. They could argue that even the most antisocial individual could use at least a few of Facebook's options for their pleasure.

In 2019, Snapchat rolled out virtual games to its users. Snapchat users can play these fun, interactive games with friends that also use the app.

Games like Bitmoji Party allow multiple users to play together. Snapchat continues to make these kinds of strides a priority. This is purposeful.

More engagement can create more opportunities for Snapchat to make money for the company and their CEO, Evan Spiegel, whose estimated worth exceeds 10 billion dollars!

In addition, there are many people that help the apps stay prominent even though they don't make a dime from the apps. Who are these people, you ask?

Us! The users. For many reasons, the people that use the apps play a factor.

Has anyone ever asked you, "What's your Instagram?" "Do you have Facebook?" "What's your Snapchat?" or any variation of the three?

This is a common occurrence. By engaging with other people and creating norms around having the apps, we, the users, help the apps remain relevant and powerful. Social media app developers want their platform to become a staple in your life in the same way that people casually mention buying things from Amazon or taking a trip to Target. This is why becoming a part of a social media apps community feels casual and effortless.

In addition, social media can be very entertaining. People post funny videos and content that keeps your eyes glued to the screen.

I can't say for sure if the experts that built these apps knew that this would occur, but what I do know is that social media's entertainment factor is heavy and oftentimes organic. People on Twitter say whatever is on their mind and sometimes their thoughts are shared by thousands.

In the past few years, Twitter has developed a culture that encourages debates. Long gone are the days of people saying whatever they want without having anyone blowing up their mentions. These discussions occur every day over varying topics; Friday morning you'll see people debating over serious issues like abortion laws or gun rights.

That same day, you'll see people debating over whether a man should pay for all the bills in his household or who is the greatest basketball player of all time. The content is diverse and eye-catching.

TikTok has found a way to create a fun platform for people of all ages, backgrounds, and interests. People on TikTok create unique videos that allow others into their mind and life. Some of the videos are funny and spontaneous while others are educational and well thought out. Either way, this content keeps people engaged and ready to return to the app.

On TikTok, it is very easy to go down a deep rabbit hole of whatever topic or hobby sparks your interest. Users sometimes inadvertently create these holes, which draw other people in and keep them on the app.

Whether we know it or not, social media users play a direct role in keeping other users hooked on the apps. As a social community, we create relationships and interact on these apps more frequently than we ever have. As more and more people join social media, this community will only grow and continue to be a notable part of our lives.

11

LISTEN & LEARN

EVERY DAY, people spend hours expressing their opinions online. We go back and forth with our Facebook friends and Twitter followers over any topic we deem worthy of our time. We argue on Clubhouse and comment on Instagram posts until our phone batteries hit 0%. We also see people make startling assumptions about other people's lives, and watch others change their opinions on social and political issues at the same time. The internet is a tricky place, but one thing we know for certain is that we can all benefit from having a listening ear.

Having a *listening* ear simply means that we are open to hearing other people's opinions before we jump to conclusions or go against them. In this chapter, we'll establish some simple actions we can take to effectively listen to others online.

If you're stuck in your ways and don't care about what other people think and feel, then skip this chapter and move on to the next one. If you want to learn and grow, keep reading.

We'll start with a scenario. We'll go back to using the green people as our subjects:

Green people are just like you and me. They work to feed their families, go to school, and want to live happy lives. But green people have faced unfair treatment in our country for a long time. Over the last 10 years, green people and their supporters have been very vocal about these injustices. Green people want to be treated fairly. Just like we do.

We have plenty of options if we want to actively assist green people offline, but let's focus on what we can do online to learn more about their experiences and help spread a positive, supportive message in favor of fairness and justice for green people.

But first, we must remember that we're on the outside looking in.

There's a solid chance that we don't truly understand what green people have been through. We may have an idea, but not the full picture. We may have relationships with green people, but that doesn't mean we understand the full scope of their struggles. We could go to school with them, hang out with them on the weekend, date them, and more, but still be oblivious to their problems. To find the right balance, we'll take the two steps below.

1) IF WE WANT TO BE A PART OF THE SOLUTION, WE CAN START BY SIMPLY LISTENING AND LEARNING. We can read articles and try to make connections with green people both within our community and online. When able, we will step outside of our comfort zone and connect with others to gain new perspectives. We can use social media to follow people that are both informed and involved. We now have the ability to engage with people all over the world. Let's use it! When green people speak, we'll hear them with a listening ear.

2) WE WILL LISTEN TO UNDERSTAND AND COMPREHEND THEIR PERSPECTIVE, *NOT* TO RESPOND. At this point, listening to understand and comprehend their perspective is more important than our opinion. This is a positive first step in ensuring we become connected to their cause and begin understanding their issues. If we take time to understand, we'll be better suited to respond with a fair opinion.

3) WE'LL REFRAIN FROM POSTING AND SUPPORTING NEGATIVE RHETORIC ONLINE.

In this case, negative rhetoric can be defined as any type of online post, whether it be text, image, or video, that causes unfair doubt toward a cause, issue, or uprising.

Here's an example. Recently, green people and their supporters have been demanding higher wages. From their perspective, their jobs do not pay enough money to support their needs. Let's say, we saw someone on our favorite social media app post a response to the green people's grievance.

That person posted statistics on rising poverty in the green community. That post includes a caption stating "They are poor because they don't work. Many of them live off the system." We agree with this perspective, so we decided to like the post.

Prior to liking that post, did we do any research to see if that information is true? If we haven't taken time to understand why poverty is rising in the green community, we should think twice before liking or supporting that post.

In addition, misinformation is running rampant online. Naturally, we have an opinion, but we should take time to test our opinion against legitimate information.

In this instance, we're buying into negative rhetoric and creating unfair doubt toward the green people's issue. We may not understand how low wages and poverty are intertwined, and we don't know if the person that made that post does either.

We also may not know which groups are the primary benefactors of government assistance. We're ignorant to this information and potentially misinformed.

Negative rhetoric doesn't help our cause. If we want to listen, understand, and potentially show support, it is imperative that we think before we post. We'll listen to what others have to say before inserting our opinion or making assumptions. If we do this, we could begin to understand that with a higher wage, fewer green people would live in poverty or require government assistance to survive.

We will take time to think about what we want to say, if we want to say anything at all. We don't have to post anything about green people or their struggles. We could listen, learn, and find other ways to show support and understanding outside of social media. Even in showing support, we don't have to post it. It's okay for us to be observant learners.

We may never join the green people's fight for justice and fairness, but at the very least, we can try to understand *why* they are fighting in the first place. We may not ever agree with their views, but we should still refrain from taking any actions, online and in Real Life, that cause them further anguish.

These concepts may seem simple, but they can be very difficult to embrace and put into action. Research shows that it can be difficult for people to change, especially as they reach adulthood. Many people aren't interested in the hard work that comes with adopting a new perspective.

While online, we can quickly find friends, family, and information that will reaffirm whatever we believe to be true.

Social media makes it very easy to have your thoughts reinforced by others. We are able to build echo chambers on our timelines.

So, what is an echo chamber? According to GCF Global, a free, online learning tool, "An echo chamber is an environment where a person only encounters information or opinions that reflect and reinforce their own. Echo chambers can create misinformation and distort a person's perspective, so they have difficulty considering opposing viewpoints and discussing complicated topics.

They're fueled in part by confirmation bias, which is the tendency to favor info that reinforces existing beliefs."

Those echo chambers give our preconceived notions power and alienate others with differing opinions. If we truly want to learn and grow, we must be willing to step outside of our comfort zone.

Understand that this type of work does not come with a shiny reward. Unlike a carnival game, there won't be a stuffed bear or cute prize to take home.

You may never receive a pat on the back for this type of personal growth. Instead, you will become a better human being for your sake and for the sake of everyone around you, which is a damn good prize.

12

THE POWER OF ANONYMITY

"Bullying disproportionally affects young people. When I was a kid, I was bullied—I could go home. When I got off the bus, I was safe. That's not the case anymore."

-Adam Mosseri, Head of Instagram, regarding his concerns around bullying on social media.

EVERY DAY, millions of people hop on social media to get the scoop on the latest gossip. If we're interested in the latest celebrity gossip, we'll probably follow The Shade Room, Baller Alert, Hollywood Unlocked, or TMZ. Even those who don't follow those pages will probably visit them from time to time to ensure they're up to date on today's gossip.

About once or twice a week, I'll look at the online gossip blogs. I'll go to The Shade Room or Baller Alert's Instagram pages and read through the comments. Sometimes the comments are funny. At times, I'll find a post and scroll through the top comments to get a laugh.

I love this kind of content when it doesn't come at someone else's expense. Oftentimes, this isn't the case. Frequently, the comments on social media's gossip pages are mean and nasty.

I've been surprised at how many cruel things I've seen people say to others. People online can be quick to judge and slow to forgive. Social media in general is vast and unpoliced for the most part— people leave nasty messages on the social media pages of celebrities almost by the minute; everything from telling actors they suck to threatening the lives of basketball players.

In 2019, Khloe Kardashian, a successful businesswoman and super celebrity, shared a post that read "Social media has made too many of you comfortable with disrespecting people and not getting punched in the mouth for it." She may be right.

Now, I am not a proponent of violence over Instagram comments, but I do believe people need to treat each other with decency, whether it be online or in Real Life. Having social media shouldn't give us the right to treat other people like crap.

Take a moment one day to scroll through two of your favorite celebrities or athletes' social media pages. You may find some weird stuff in the comments. LeBron James is my favorite basketball player. I admire his work ethic on and off the court. I have a hard time imagining why someone would truly *hate* one of my idols, but I know it happens. I recently went through LeBron's Instagram comments on multiple posts from 2018 to 2021.

Depending on the post, I found a mix of responses. If it was strictly basketball, people were mostly complimentary. People love leaving thumbs up and GOAT emojis on his pictures when he's winning a championship, dunking on somebody, or hanging with his friends and family.

On the opposite end, if LeBron posts anything that seems socially or politically charged, a whole different world of comments opens up. Some people are very open in Lebron's comments about the fact that they'd rather see him shoot a jump shot than wear a Black Lives Matter T-Shirt. Many of these commenters have private accounts and post very few pictures of themselves, their friends, or family.

I don't care to write about everything that these people said in *The Chosen One's* comments, but I'll leave you with this:

Social media provides people with a unique opportunity to say whatever they want with little to no consequences.

Remember this word. Anonymity. According to Merriam-Webster, anonymity can be defined as the quality or state of being anonymous.

Whether right or wrong, anonymity is a privilege we're able to exercise online. The Pew Research Center has spent a considerable amount of time surveying Americans on their opinions about social media. An excerpt from one of their 2020 studies is below. Check it out:

"Anonymity is seen as a facilitating factor in encouraging the spread of harassment online"

"Users increasingly see the internet as a place that facilitates anonymity. Some 86 percent of online adults feel that the internet allows people to be more anonymous than is true offline. This represents a notable increase from the 62 percent who said this in Pew Research Center's 2014 survey. And this ability to be anonymous online is often tied to the issue of online harassment.

Roughly half of those who have been harassed online (54 percent) say their most recent incident involved a stranger and/or someone whose real identity they did not know. More broadly, 89 percent of Americans say the ability to post anonymously online enables people to be cruel to or harass one another."

These data points are very important for us to understand. It is clear that we *know* the ability to be anonymous online gives us an opportunity to interact with other people in a unique way. But we also *know* that this anonymity can be used to harass others.

Many of us understand that being able to hide behind a phone gives us power, even if we use that power solely to harm other people.

If we want, we can scroll through Khloe Kardashian's Instagram pictures and think of the meanest possible comment to type.

You may be thinking to yourself "Why on earth would I do that? That's not right."

Or it's quite possible that you've actually done this before, thought to do it, or at least understand *why* someone would do it. Despite where you fall on this spectrum, it's clear that this type of behavior is an everyday reality of the internet.

Anonymity allows us to be whoever we want to be while we're online. We can interact with others in a different way online than we can in Real Life. As long as we don't forget to pay AT&T for the Wi-fi, we can do this all day, every day.

If I wanted to, I could steal pictures from my little brother's Facebook page. I could make an account with his name and pretend to be him. In Real Life, it would be much harder for me to impersonate my brother. I am much taller and much more handsome than he is.

Nobody on this planet would believe I'm him! Online, however, it would be pretty easy, especially if I had access to his personal information. It would be a piece of cake.

If you haven't, check out MTV's, *Catfish: The TV Show*. *Catfish* chronicles the stories of everyday people that are in relationships and friendships with people online that they've never met. On the show, the guests look for answers to the many questions they have regarding their online lover who may be "catfishing" them. The show typically ends with the guests finding an answer to their questions. Oftentimes, they are being lied to and catfished.

Pretending to be someone else has become a norm on the internet. Social media is no exception. Every day, someone, somewhere, is masquerading online as someone else.

There are various reasons people pretend to be others online— whether to make money through scamming or to find love, the reasons for this behavior are vast.

I've heard horror stories from women whose pictures were used by strangers for dating apps and social media sites.

I can't imagine how intrusive and odd that must feel—knowing someone is pretending to be you and striking up conversations with complete strangers about Lord knows what.

Anonymity, coupled with social media's unique landscape, is a breeding ground for harassment. Once again:

Social media provides people with a unique opportunity to say whatever they want with little to no consequences.

It's on us to decide how we treat others online. If we want to bully people all day, we can. If we want to show people love all day, we can. There are plenty of options. I believe that the best option would be to refrain from harassing other people online. Many of us can identify online harassment as a problem so I would rather be a part of the solution. I don't think anyone has anything to gain by mistreating others, even if it is through a screen. Online harassment isn't harmless.

Words can hurt!

We must remember there's a thin line between jokes and harassment. From harassing people in the LGBTQ community to threatening violence against people we've never met, none of it is acceptable and we should do our part to end it.

Ultimately, social media is meant to be enjoyed. Have fun with it! Tweet your jokes. Post that funny picture. Create that TikTok video to Megan Thee Stallion's new song even though you can't dance. Argue with strangers on Instagram over which zodiac sign is the most toxic.

It's fine by me. Who doesn't love scrolling through their timeline to find a laugh?

The laughs are endless on social media, and many of us enjoy it. We enjoy the quick access to comedic relief and content that makes us smile. We can have fun in our digital lives without hurting other people, so just do it.

13

YOUR TIMELINE ISN'T A REFLECTION OF THE REAL WORLD

"We live in a world with few boundaries and a lot of access. There are so many internet therapists, comment critics, and experts with no expertise. Our reality can be warped because it's based on a personalized algorithm. It shows us whatever truths we are searching for, and that's dangerous."

-Beyoncé, on present day internet culture.

LISTEN, there's a *very* good chance your timeline isn't a reflection of the real world. Let's say you only follow people from your hometown. Most of these people are friends and family you grew up with or classmates from high school. As I've mentioned, I grew up in Detroit. If I only followed people from Detroit, my timeline would reflect a very small set of views, opinions, and beliefs. It would also lack ethnic diversity, especially if I only connected with people from my community.

If you only followed people from your hometown, what would your timeline look like? Would you be connected to people that don't share your religious or spiritual beliefs? What about people of different backgrounds and ethnicities?

If your social media pages are anything like mine, your timeline is a bubble. It's insulated and likely doesn't reflect a full range of views, opinions, and beliefs. Since many communities across America are often segregated, there's a chance that your timeline lacks ethnic diversity.

My "Detroit" timeline doesn't reflect rural America. It doesn't reflect the views of Asian Americans and reflects the views of very few Caucasian Americans, Latino Americans, and Arab Americans.

Now, this is through no fault of mine as I built my timeline naturally by following my friends, family, and interests. I didn't purposefully refrain from following people in these communities.

Instead, it happened naturally as these people weren't in my community as I grew into adulthood. When thinking of your timeline, are there any groups of people that are left out? Are most of the people you're following of the same race or ethnicity or background? What about their financial status?

So, why is this important? We'll establish two truths to answer that question:

1. We must understand that regardless of the social media platform we use, if we don't create a timeline that invites diversity and differing viewpoints, our timeline will be insulated. It will be an echo chamber. Our timeline will be more likely to reaffirm what we believe and feel than to discredit it. By diverse, I mean consisting of people, organizations, and outlets that have differing views and

opinions. If we want a greater feel for the world, we must look for it.

2. Gaining a pulse on the real world through social media can be very, very tricky. It's tricky because many of us curate our timelines based on our interests. If we're interested in connecting with family and friends, there's a strong chance we will follow them. If we're interested in buying houses, we'll probably follow real estate agents, well-known real estate moguls, successful investors, and outlets that help us learn more about purchasing a home.

Curating our timelines this way can be useful because it gives us an opportunity to build our timeline around our interests. Our passions are at our fingertips!

But on the opposite end, we create a bubble. We create an environment that reflects only what we want it to reflect, which is not necessarily a true depiction of the world we live in.

Also, some people do not choose to voice their opinions on social media, but the choices they make can impact the world.

In 2016, I remember scrolling through Twitter as the presidential debates took place. I paid close attention to my timeline and the words of the candidates. I *distinctly* remember the moment Donald Trump's "law and order" rhetoric surfaced when asked about Black Lives Matter and police brutality toward black people.

Many, many people that I keep up with on Twitter and Facebook took issue with those comments and other statements he made leading up to the election.

I was confident going into that Wednesday morning, Donald Trump would've been on his way back to *The Apprentice*, firing celebrities instead of leading America from the White House. To my surprise, Trump became president. My drive to work felt very weird that morning. I thought to myself, "How did this happen? People don't like him!" The news I watched predicted that he would lose. My Twitter followers said that he would lose. My friends said that he would lose. My family said that he would lose. *I* said that he would lose!

In this instance from my Real Life, my *community* shared a similar belief: *Donald Trump wasn't fit to be president and he won't win.* Well, he won.

Today, we can apply our two truths to this situation. At that time, my timeline was in no way a reflection of the real world. I didn't see a lot of support for Trump, and that's probably because I didn't welcome or look for it. Also, there were and are people who support Trump's thoughts and views that don't feel a need to express those opinions on social media.

During the 2016 election many people voted, but everyone *didn't* tell the world who they planned to and did ultimately vote for. Everyone didn't make a status about their love for Donald Trump or admiration for Hillary Clinton.

Let's make something clear: We're less likely to be shocked when we understand that the information coming across our screens is catered to us.

If I knew this in 2016, I may not have been super surprised when Donald Trump became the president of the United States.

Take a second to think about today's hot topic. What is one major issue or concern that many people you interact with on social media *seem* to agree about? Take about three minutes to think it over. Write it down below.

_____

_____

_____

_____

_____

Done? Remember this: Many people you follow may agree on that issue, but that doesn't mean most of the country, let alone the world, does. Unless you purposefully seek out diverse views on issues, you'll never find them. Often, what you see on social media reflects what you *choose* to see—the people you *choose* to follow and what makes you comfortable.

If different perspectives are what you desire, follow people that don't agree with you. Give your timeline a little room to make you uncomfortable. Follow that well-known political correspondent from the network you never watch because you don't agree with them AT ALL.

Follow that politician you can't stand to hear talk. There's a good chance these people will say something you don't like! They may make you want to hit that unfollow button!

But there's also a chance that by trying to understand their opinion, you will gain a greater understanding of people outside your community.

There's a chance that these people's views will give you a unique opportunity to view the world from a different angle. Remember, there are people that think exactly like that well-known person you don't agree with.

These people may or may not post about it, but they absolutely exist, and they are just as real as you and me.

By "understand," I don't mean "agree with." Understanding means to comprehend. In this case, there is power in understanding people, even if you don't agree with them one bit.

Recently, I followed a few people I don't agree with on Twitter. At times, their views piss me off. At the same time, I'm glad to see what they think because there are other people who have similar thoughts and sometimes those people have power and influence.

This information gives me a greater feel for the *other* side of America—for the people that view the world differently than I do. For the people that I once thought (and maybe still do) were crazy!

In addition, we must also understand that information reporting has changed rapidly and unexpectedly due to the rise of social media. The world of journalism has been turned on its head.

In the early 2000s, you had to have some sort of credentials or platform to be seen as a legitimate news source. Whether it be a news show, radio broadcast, or journalism degree, in some way or another the people that were trusted to report on the news held these positions, titles, and accolades.

Today, anyone with two thumbs can create a Twitter account and begin sharing information. They don't need to be validated as credible sources to do this.

Whether this is good or bad is a topic for another day, but the truth is that social media has created *more* room for misinformation. Misinformation has the ability to travel at the same rate as, if not faster than, true information.

In 2014, I received my bachelor's degree in Journalism along with a concentration in Media Marketing from Michigan State University (Go Green!).

In journalism school, I learned rules, standards, and codes of conduct for journalists. I was taught the do's and don'ts of information reporting and sharing. I had to read *Ethics of Journalism* by Ron H Smith and *Public Affairs Reporting Now, News of, by and for the People* by G.Michael Killenberg among other books that emphasized the "rules" of the journalism game.

Today, many people sharing information online did not receive this type of training. People are able to post, share, tweet, and retweet information, regardless of the information's validity.

This is becoming a huge issue. So much so, Twitter has begun attaching labels and warnings to information that could be seen as misleading or untrue.

But here's the kicker: Just because someone has a degree, title, accolades, or large platform, that doesn't automatically make them a fair or reputable source. People with an education in a field aren't guaranteed to be *competent* in that field. In some cases, these people are guilty of spreading misinformation as well.

If I wanted to, I could start a YouTube channel today about climate change. I could tweet out data that *looked* accurate and call myself a climate change expert that has dedicated my life to saving the environment.

In theory, if I made myself look the part, people may post, share, tweet, and retweet information they've received from me even though I have no idea what I'm talking about! Think about it. Does the post below look truthful to you?

> "The Climate Institution of America estimated that 20 percent of the Arctic will melt within the next 50 years."

Well, it's not. But it sure looks the part.

What about this one?

> "Asbestos is a dangerous, naturally occurring mineral that is harmful to human beings. Moderna's COVID-19 vaccine contains traces of Asbestos."

This one is partially true. Yes, Asbestos is a dangerous mineral that can hurt human beings, but there is no legitimate data or reporting stating it is in Moderna's COVID-19 vaccine, or any other vaccine for that matter.

This type of misinformation has become a constant online. These days, false information, truthful information and somewhat truthful information all exist within the same space. This phenomenon can lead one to question the information they see, even if that information is accurate and from a legitimate source.

On the opposite end, this phenomenon can lead one to wholeheartedly believe the information they see without questioning its validity.

Finding accurate reporting can be tricky. But there are plenty of fair, honest journalists out there. These people are dedicated to their craft and invest the time and energy to report the truth. When able, seek out trusted news sources and outlets with proven track records.

When in doubt, do your own research. Seek out unbiased sources in an effort to gain greater perspective. Don't be afraid to question the posts you see, regardless of where it comes from.

I've tried this and it's given me a greater feel for not only other opinions but also where my opinions lie on critical topics. Don't buy into the idea that any of the major news outlets only report false information.

This isn't the case for CNN, MSNBC, Fox News, or NPR. Understand that it's fine to read and watch different news sources to find out where the truth lies. For example, you can watch both MSNBC and Fox News, but not just one of the two. You could also listen to NPR. A balanced media diet is healthy!

14

DATING APPS ARE THE PRESENT AND THE FUTURE

"Love today's gone digital

And it's messing with my health"

-J.Cole, Photograph

ONE OF THE most peculiar effects of the rise of the internet is the explosion of the dating app. In early 2021, the CEO of Bumble, Whitney Wolfe, became the youngest female CEO to take a company public. Around this same time, Forbes estimated that Whitney Wolfe was worth well over half a billion dollars and counting! Bumble, the dating app that asks women to make the first move, had roughly 5 million users in the US in 2019.

Bumble markets that it's able to assist users who are looking for romantic relationships, platonic friendships, and business partnerships.

Recently, one of my good friends joined Bumble. He is a tall, nice-looking guy, a former college athlete, and someone that I saw women gravitate toward. On the eve of his 30th birthday, he started swiping on the app in an effort to find "the one." He told me that he was narrowing his potential pool of women down to four as he showed me his Bumble profile. His "Final Four," as I like to call them, were all very attractive, educated, and seemingly outgoing women.

Ten years ago, I probably would've found this behavior to be odd. I would've asked, "What do you mean you're trying to meet your girlfriend on an app?" I would've told him "You're the man! You don't need an app to meet women!"

But today, dating online is not odd behavior at all. In fact, the number of people leaning on apps to meet others is rising.

The dating app has evolved and changed since Tinder called us to the online "streets" when it launched in 2012.

The dating app is the present and the future.

Online dating has become a billion-dollar industry and continues to grow. The internet has forever changed the way people meet. Whether it be for dating or for friendship, the internet allows us to connect with people we want to have in our lives. It is important to realize, however, that dating apps are, in fact, social media apps.

At their core, they create an environment for us to meet new people and build relationships with them. Like most social media apps, popular dating apps Tinder, Bumble, and Hinge are free to join. Each app is different in some way or another, but they all ask us to provide pictures of ourselves and information about our interests, personality, preferences, education, politics, religion, and more.

As dating apps continue to influence the world, pop culture has found a way to fit them into our movies, shows, music, and more.

One of my favorite shows is *Rick & Morty*. There are many hilarious episodes, but one in particular stood out to me while writing this chapter. In "The Old Man and the Seat," Jerry, one of the show's main characters, decides to work with a strange alien to develop an app even though the alien has "do not develop an app with me" written across his forehead.

The app, Loverbuddz, is a dating app that encourages users to find their soulmate. Jerry's daughter, Summer, falls right into the app's deadly trap. She begins to blindly chase after chaotic romantic relationships, no matter how the previous one ended.

Summer jumps from partner to partner, with her mother, Beth, frantically chasing her every step of the way. The episode ends with the app beginning to show ads, which immediately turns everyone off.

Rick and Morty is an animated comedy, but their app, "Loverbuddz, isn't that farfetched. The original *culture* of dating apps like Tinder was to keep making connections. Keep swiping. And if you run out of matches? Don't worry, the app will find more matches. There will always be more matches.

Dating apps can be a positive experience for many, but we must remain careful while using them for various reasons. For this chapter, we'll focus on only one of those reasons:

Dating apps have the ability to create the illusion of infinite options, or as I like to call them, Infinite Matches.

On dating apps, it is *very* easy to meet someone new if the last interaction doesn't work. This isn't necessarily a *constructive* use of our time when it comes to our mentality while dating online. You can find "the one," again and again and again.

On Tinder, which is essentially the "OG" of dating apps, you can swipe and swipe and swipe until your index finger goes numb. Under these circumstances, people can become *disposable*.

Think about it. If you can match with another potential partner in three seconds, why should you care about the last one? If you're messaging someone and you don't like their tone...oh well. You can unmatch them and message someone else in the blink of an eye. You have more options than a Cheesecake Factory menu.

If we're not careful, dating apps can begin to feel more like a game than an actual interaction with another human being. This can be dangerous.

We can use these apps as a tool to jump from relationship to relationship, if we choose to. Understand that dating apps are a unique form of social media that create a pathway for us to date, 24/7.

As someone who has used Tinder, I am guilty of this. I'll be honest. I've had a few "Summer" moments of my own. More than once, I've swiped from woman to woman. While swiping, I wasn't thinking about any long-term dating goals, if they even existed for me at that time.

I am 100 percent guilty of using dating apps to serial date, which often led to my relationships going downhill as quickly as they started. At that time, I exercised my infinite options a bit too often. I abused it.

In time, I realized that the constant swiping and matching wasn't healthy behavior, and constantly having options via an app didn't actually help me in the long run. Exercising the ability to continue swiping wasn't the best choice for me and may not be the best choice for you either.

For the sake of our sanity, we need to acknowledge that Infinite Matches don't *truly* exist. Yes, you could date everyone you meet online in theory, but that would be an awful experience for you and probably for them as well. Eventually, you would get tired of asking people what their favorite food is and how many siblings they have.

If you use multiple dating apps, I can 100 percent guarantee that you'll never run out of matches, but there is a strong chance you'll run out of patience, attention, and time to entertain these people.

Again, the dating app has changed considerably and continues to change. The experts at these companies have figured out winning algorithms to create an engaging user experience. Apps like Hinge tend to lean toward encouraging people to develop relationships as opposed to continually dating online.

That's great for someone looking for a serious commitment, but the data shows most people will not find long-term relationships on dating apps or websites.

According to eHarmony, one of the premier dating websites, only 20 percent of Americans in committed relationships began online. eHarmony reported that people are most likely to find love through a friend.

Understand that dating apps are here to stay and will likely grow in popularity in part due to how we interact with one another due to the impact of COVID-19. According to Grit Daily, the number of daily active users on dating apps increased during the pandemic. There's a chance that more and more people will look for relationships online as they spend less time around humans. At this point, using them isn't unnatural, but it should be monitored.

Remember these apps can be unhealthy if you abuse them. If you find yourself on too many dating apps or any app too often, take a breath and put the phone down. Same goes for any online dating website. Take a step back when you need to. Enjoy yourself, but don't take it overboard!

Oh, and for the guys out there, don't feel weird the next time you ask a girl to set you up with her friend. Research shows that's the best way to find love!

15

PUT YOUR PHONE DOWN!

IF YOU HAD TO GUESS, how much time in a *day* do you spend on social media? Think about that for a moment.

Now, how much time in a *week* do you spend on social media? Spend a moment thinking about that as well. Feel free to write down your guesses for both questions here.

_____

_____

_____

_____

_____

Now, if you're able to, find the actual data. See if the device you use to access social media allows you to see your "Screen Time," which is also known as "Digital Wellbeing" on some devices. Take your time finding this information. We're in no rush here. If you don't have the data, roll with your best guess. Feel free to take notes on your findings here.

_____

_____

_____

_____

_____

_____

So, what did you learn? Are you spending hours at a time on social media? Are certain apps taking up more of your time than others?

You may have not learned anything as you could be in the know regarding your screen time, but if you're like me you *did* learn a thing or two. I learned that I spend roughly 3.5 hours a day on social media, with a slight increase on the weekend.

I found that Fridays are the biggest social media days for me (don't tell my job!).

I also discovered I spend about 3.2 hours a week on Instagram, 2.5 hours on Twitter, and about 2.25 hours texting.

According to *Whatagraph*, a data-driven marketing reporting tool, adults spent 90 minutes per day on social media in 2012. In 2020, adults spent about three hours per day on social media.

Some researchers believe adults spend closer to two and a half hours per day on social media.

Either way, that's a major amount of time spent online, and I'm no exception. My 3.5 hours per day is above the average. This average time spent on social media continues to rise year over year.

So, the question remains, what do you do with your data and why does it matter?

A temporary detox from the noise of social media has positive benefits. If your usage numbers are as high as mine, you should put the phone down!

Here's why: as we discussed earlier, social media use can lead to anxiety, depravity, and unfair comparisons between your Real Life and the online lives of others, among other concerning, unhealthy consequences. We must be careful about how much we expose ourselves to these emotions and feelings.

Some of us are more susceptible to being negatively impacted by high social media use than others, but either way, we must understand the potential impact it can have on our mental health.

An extreme amount of social media use can be dangerous, especially if you're unaware of it. Remember, if it doesn't serve a specific purpose (business, school, networking, etc) then you must control your engagement.

Let's put a healthy number to our social media use.

A high amount of social media use can be defined as exceeding three hours a day.

Keep in mind that adults currently maintain a daily average that falls between two and a half to three hours.

If we average three hours a day on social media, we're likely to reach or exceed 1,000 hours spent on social media every year.

If we're thinking big picture, social media usage will only continue to increase. You may spend four, five, six, or seven hours a day on social media. If that's you, you're not alone. Humans are spending more and more time online. We're more connected than we've ever been, and that won't change!

At this point, it is OK to be an average user. But if you're exceeding three hours a day, put the phone down. One exception being if you use social media for a specific purpose like the ones mentioned earlier.

If you fall into that group, your data is more than likely a mix of *working* time and *recreation* time online, which can become hard to separate.

If that's not the case, log off and give yourself a breather. Do whatever you have to do to ease up a bit, especially if you have any inclination that social media is negatively impacting your mental health.

Have you ever tried detoxing from social media? Logging off for an extended period is actually very difficult for most people. We're stuck in our habits and glued to our phones, making it hard to put the phone down; for many of us, swiping down our timeline happens naturally and often.

We do it without really thinking about a purpose or goal.

If you've ever deleted social media apps from your phone, you've probably opened your phone to visit them before remembering you were taking a break!

I once tried to quit Instagram. Slowly but surely, I found myself spending too much time on Twitter!

Soon after, I left Twitter for Facebook, but I got off quickly after scrolling my timeline and seeing my shirtless father cooking gumbo. You could argue that I was chasing my daily social media "hit."

According to TheHealthy.com, most people feel stress and anxiety when they delete their social media accounts, but those feelings fall off after a while. The stress and anxiety in the beginning explains why taking a break can be so tough. You will likely feel tempted to hop back on those apps and return to your normal routine.

In addition, the website reported you'll get more sleep! More rest sounds good, right? A bit more energy during the day could help us all.

Sometimes, we need to be still. Log out, take a breath, and connect with something that doesn't involve a screen, which can be a challenge. But it is very possible. There is more than one way to do this. A few tips are below.

1) Try deleting or hiding your apps during the time of day you're busiest. If you're like most, this would be the morning to late afternoon. If done consistently, this will allow you time to be productive during the day and enjoy social media in the evening.

2) Delete or hide your apps for days at a time. As we mentioned, this can be challenging, but well worth it. A few days off of social media won't kill you. When you return, the online world will still be in full swing and fully capable of getting you back up to speed.

3) If social media is truly impacting your life in a negative way, strongly consider getting off of it entirely. Do not let the online world turn your Real Life upside down. It's not worth it. Delete the apps and do not return to them until you feel mentally prepared for their impact on your life.

When you're exercising these options, you may feel like you're "missing out" on whatever is happening online. Do your best to calm those feelings. The truth is, you don't need to be in the know about every event as soon as it happens. Important information will find its way to you even if you aren't on social media.

Screens are thoroughly embedded in our culture. So much so that many students in the US and beyond were able to attend school virtually for well over a year due to the pandemic. These students learned through the power of technology, which obviously includes screens.

If you think screens aren't powerful, ask anyone with small children if they've ever turned CocoMelon on their TV or tablet then sat their kids in front of that screen. Soon enough, their children go into a trance as they are hypnotized by the bright colors and fun songs.

From our laptops to our phones, screens have found a way to invade our existence. Drawing back can be tough, but just remember that a temporary break won't hurt you. You don't need to be in the know regarding everything happening online. You don't need to see every picture coming down your timeline. If it's important enough, it will find a way to reach you.

16

YOUR MIRAGE

As you can tell by now, a lot of *Mirage* revolves around the things we see online that may or may not be true. As the internet has grown, the room for us to receive confusing messages has done the same; the internet is a noisy place, and the truth has become harder to see and feel.

The *Mirage* I look into shows me material goods, fancy degrees, successful businesses, cool clothes, and fast cars. At times, I have to remind myself that social media creates an illusion of who actually has these things and what it takes to get them. Your *Mirage* could be completely different from mine.

Yours could be a picture-perfect family, a huge house, a dream job, fun vacations, or validation from your friends and family. These things are attainable, but we must separate what we can achieve from what the internet tells us are *"goals."* By goals, I mean the things we're told we should or need to strive for even though those things may not be as they appear. Check yourself in the same way that I do. Take a deep breath and remember that you're running your own race. Your path is uniquely yours.

Take time to think about what your *Mirage* is. If you're reading this, you have one. There is some position, situation, or opportunity that you want to reach, but what you see online may skew your view of it. Whatever that is, want it for your own fulfillment and no one else's validation.

If the pressures of social media and the internet are becoming too much to bear, consider seeking help. Consider speaking with a professional to help you through whatever you're feeling. Remember, your mental health is yours to care for.

In recent years, I've seen an uptick in influential people attesting to the need for our community to seek professional help for our issues.

I went to therapy for years and I'm a firm believer that we can all benefit from it.

On the next page, you'll find some mental-health resources available in the US and beyond. Please share these resources as there may be someone in your life in need.

Also, I would love it if you could leave your honest review. Reviews can greatly impact the success of independent, self-published books like this one. I would truly appreciate any feedback you're willing to give.

Lastly, please feel free to stay connected with me for more *Mirage* content via the platforms listed below.

Website: www.themiragebook.com

Facebook: https://www.facebook.com/Mirage-The-Truth-About-Social-Media-145237531032349/

Instagram: https://www.instagram.com/miragebook_/

Tyler's LinkedIn: https://www.linkedin.com/in/tyler-hendon-b8282a35/

Tyler's Email: tylerhendon7@gmail.com

MENTAL HEALTH RESOURCES

NATIONAL SUICIDE PREVENTION LIFELINE

Website: https://suicidepreventionlifeline.org/

Contact: (800-273-8255)

MENTAL HEALTH IS HEALTH

Website: https://www.mentalhealthishealth.us/

Contact: Text ACTION to 741-741 to connect with a trainer counselor for free.

THE DEPRESSION PROJECT

Website: https://thedepressionproject.com/

Contact: Contact@thedepressionproject.com

SAMSHA (SUBSTANCE ABUSE AND MENTAL HEALTH SERVICES ADMINISTRATION)

Website: https://www.samhsa.gov/

Contact: (800-662-4357)

VETERANS' CRISIS LINE

Website: https://www.veteranscrisisline.net/

Contact: (800-273-8255) and Press 1

NATIONAL INSTITUTE OF MENTAL HEALTH

Website: https://www.nimh.nih.gov/

Contact: (866-615-6464)

DEDICATION

I toyed with the idea of writing this book for nearly a year. Even though I knew that I wanted to write it, I wasn't particularly motivated to get it done. In the middle of 2020, I experienced a huge loss. Unbeknownst to me, that loss gave me the drive I needed to write this book.

In May of that year, I lost my oldest sister, Ewanda. Her passing affected me deeply. I was a bit lost. The pain and confusion I felt lingered in my mind for months. After a period of mourning and connecting with my faith, I was able to hone in on two beliefs:

1. Life is short. We have a finite amount of time to do whatever we're put here to do.
2. Our dreams are real and, if we're lucky, we'll get a chance to chase them.

These two simple yet important beliefs led to me writing this book. I decided to chase my dream of becoming an independent, successful, self-published author. I decided that I would use whatever time I have on this planet to create the best book I could possibly write.

I would like to thank my mother, father, aunt, and grandmother for their wisdom and love. I would like to thank my close friends and family for their support and loyalty. I would like to thank my big sister for seeing my light. Lastly, I would like to thank God for giving me the time, money, and resources to create this book.

My sister lived a beautiful life. During her life, she found tremendous success as an entrepreneur and was awarded the Spirit of Detroit Award due to her investment in our community. She impacted the world in a positive way and helped many people.

I hope and pray that Ewanda is proud of my work and she sees that I've done my best to give my gifts to the world, in the same way she did.

My hope is that *Mirage* impacted you in a positive way. I wanted to provide some gems—a few pieces of knowledge that will make you a better version of yourself.

Thank you for supporting my work. It truly means a lot to me, my family, and my community.

Tyler

ABOUT THE AUTHOR

Tyler was born and raised in Detroit, Michigan. He is an entrepreneur, business consultant, writer, public speaker, and experienced human resources professional. Tyler received his bachelor's degree in Journalism along with a concentration in Media Marketing from Michigan State University. In May of 2018, Tyler received two Human Resources Management certifications while continuing his education at Emory University. In his spare time, Tyler volunteers for Hands on Atlanta, a nonprofit dedicated to serving Metro Atlanta, and HERO for Children, a nonprofit dedicated to bettering the lives of children who have been impacted by HIV and Aids. Tyler currently resides in Atlanta, Georgia, and he frequently visits his family in Detroit, Michigan and Chicago, Illinois.

NOTES

1. "Number of Employers Using Social Media to Screen Candidates at All-Time High, Finds Latest CareerBuilder Study," PR Newswire, News Releases, June 15, 2017, https://www.prnewswire.com/news-releases/number-of-employers-using-social-media-to-screen-candidates-at-all-time-high-finds-latest-careerbuilder-study-300474228.html
2. "70% of employers are snooping candidates' social media profiles," Career Builder, Career and Job Advice, June 15, 2017, https://www.careerbuilder.com/advice/social-media-survey-2017
3. "Proof That No One Really Cares About Our Social Media Posts," Psychology Today, Blog, Tech Happy Life, March 13, 2019, https://www.psychologytoday.com/us/blog/tech-happy-life/201903/proof-no-one-really-cares-about-our-social-media-posts
4. "6 Reasons Why Tinder Should Be Treated As Another Social Media App," Hot in Social Media, Medium, June 14, 2017, https://hotinsocialmedia.medium.com/6-reasons-

why-tinder-should-be-treated-as-another-social-media-app-4eee916b1d71

5. "How Sean Rad turned the hunt for love into an addictive game," MoneyWeek, Profiles, June 4, 2014, https://moneyweek.com/323117/how-sean-rad-turned-the-hunt-for-love-into-an-addictive-game

6. Spokeo, Spokeo.com, "About."

7. Peoplefinders, Peoplefinders.com, "People Search."

8. "Study: The ever-changing landscape of dating apps," Grit Daily, June 28, 2020, https://gritdaily.com/study-ever-changing-landscape-dating-apps/

9. "These Are the Best Dating Apps for Marriage, According to Data," The Knot, Content, June 09, 2021, https://www.theknot.com/content/best-dating-apps-for-marriage#:~:text=Tinder,the%20most%20popular%20dating%20app

10. "10 Online Dating Statistics You Should Know," eharmony, March 18, 2021, https://www.eharmony.com/online-dating-statistics/

11. "Why Tinder Is The Worst Social-Media Platform In The World!," Johnny Stork, MSc, Medium, July 09, 2019, https://johnnystork.medium.com/why-tinder-is-the-worst-social-media-platform-in-the-world-3a086e216dac

12. "What happens to your brain when you get a like on instagram," Business Insider, Science, March 25, 2017, https://www.google.com/amp/s/www.businessinsider.com/what-happens-to-your-brain-like-instagram-dopamine-2017-3%3famp

13. "How much time do people spend on social media," whatagraph, blog, August 31, 2020, https://whatagraph.com/blog/articles/how-much-time-do-people-spend-on-social-media#mcetoc_1eh2d0tfuc2

14. "6 Ways Social Media Affects Our Mental Health," Forbes, Alice G. Walton, June 30, 2017, https://www.

forbes.com/sites/alicegwalton/2017/06/30/a-run-down-of-social-medias-effects-on-our-mental-health/?sh=17456b1e2e5a

15. "Is social media bad for you? The evidence and the unknowns," BBC, Future, January 4, 2018, https://www.bbc.com/future/article/20180104-is-social-media-bad-for-you-the-evidence-and-the-unknowns

16. Adam Alter, *Irresistible: The Rise Of Addictive Technology And the Business of Keeping Us Hooked,* (New York: Penguin Press, 2018)

17. LifeLock, Lifelock.com, "How LifeLock Works."

18. Dictionary.com, Definitions, "Materialism."

19. "COVID-19 Demographic and Economic Resources," US Census Bureau COVID-19 Site, https://covid19.census.gov/

20. Adam Mosseri, "Head Of Instagram Adam Mosseri On Combating Hate Speech, Bots, Racism + Algorithm Myths," Interview by Breakfast Club Power 105.1FM, July 2, 2021, Video, https://youtu.be/WRlbfPam6Fw

21. "How Do Social Media Apps Make Money," Press Release, The Silicon Review, June 03, 2019, https://thesiliconreview.com/2019/06/how-do-social-media-apps-make-money

22. "How Facebook, Twitter, Social Media Make Money From You," Business, Investopedia, February 7, 2020, https://www.investopedia.com/stock-analysis/032114/how-facebook-twitter-social-media-make-money-you-twtr-lnkd-fb-goog.aspx

23. "INSTAGRAM AND COPYRIGHT — WHAT ARE THE TERMS OF USE?," Copyrightlaws.com, January 11, 2021, https://www.copyrightlaws.com/instagram-and-copyright/

24. "Challenge The Echo Chamber | Adam Greenwood | TEDxRoyalTunbridgeWells, "Youtube, TEDx, Adam

Greenwood, April 9, 2019, Video, https://www.youtube.com/watch?v=UKyFL389qe8

25. "What is an Echo Chamber," Digital Media Literacy, GCF Global, June 18, 2019, Video, https://edu.gcfglobal.org/en/digital-media-literacy/what-is-an-echo-chamber/1/

26. "Updating our approach to misleading information," Twitter, Product, May 11, 2020, https://blog.twitter.com/en_us/topics/product/2020/updating-our-approach-to-misleading-information

27. "Orlowski, Jeff,director, 2020. *The Social Dilemma*. Netflix. https://www.netflix.com/title/81254224

28. "Systemic Equity Assessment: A Picture of Racial Equity Challenges and Opportunities in Loudoun County Public School District", The Equity Collaborative, Loudoun County Public School District, June 6, 2019, https://www.lcps.org/cms/lib/VA01000195/Centricity/domain/60/equity_initiative_documents/LCPS_Equity_Report_FINALReport12_2_19.pdf

29. "Beyoncé's Evolution", Harper's BAZAAR, Features, August 10, 2021, https://www.harpersbazaar.com/culture/features/a37039502/beyonce-evolution-interview-2021/

30. "G Herbo launches mental health initiative to provide free therapy sessions and more", The FADER, MUSIC, July 31, 2020, https://www.thefader.com/2020/07/31/g-herbo-mental-health-initiative-free-therapy

31. "G Herbo buys his old school, converts it to community center", REVOLT, News, September 24, 2020, https://www.revolt.tv/news/2020/9/24/21454440/g-herbo-buys-old-school-converts-community-center

32. "Rapper Nipsey Hussle gives back to local school", Youtube, KTLA 5, November 30, 2018, Video, https://www.youtube.com/watch?v=qgX2BLHRCqI

33. "Nipsey Hussle planned meeting with LAPD to discuss

ways to fight gang violence", CBS News, News, April 1, 2019, https://www.cbsnews.com/news/nipsey-hussle-shot-dead-lapd-meeting-fighting-gang-violence-2019-04-01/

34. "Kanye West Defends Comments That Slavery Was a Choice: 'We Can't Be Mentally Imprisoned for Another 400 Years", Billboard, News, May, 1, 2018, https://www.billboard.com/articles/news/8430171/kanye-west-defends-tmz-comments-slavery-was-a-choice

35. J.Cole. *"Photograph"*. Track 3 on *KOD*. Dreamville, Inc. Roc Nation Records. April 20, 2018.

36. "The 'BBL effect': Plastic surgeons say they're seeing record numbers of patients as people look to lift their bodies — and their booties — out of the pandemic", Business Insider, Healthcare, July, 27, 2021, https://www.businessinsider.com/plastic-surgeons-seeing-record-patients-after-covid-19-bbl-popularity-2021-7

37. "The $5,000 quest for the perfect butt", Vox, The Goods, 22598377, Aug, 02, 2021,

38. https://www.vox.com/the-goods/22598377/bbl-brazilian-butt-lift-miami-cost-tiktok

39. "Investigation: How TikTok's Algorithm Figures Out Your Deepest Desires" , The Wall Street Journal, Video, July , 21, 2021, https://www.wsj.com/video/series/inside-tiktoks-highly-secretive-algorithm/investigation-how-tiktok-algorithm-figures-out-your-deepest-desires/6C0C2040-FF25-4827-8528-2BD6612E3796?mod=hp_lead_pos5&mod=article_inline

40. Merriam-webster.com, Search for a Word, "Algorithm."

Made in the USA
Columbia, SC
08 January 2022